The Moral Foundation
of Democracy

The Moral Foundation
of Democracy

By JOHN H. HALLOWELL

 THE UNIVERSITY OF CHICAGO PRESS

CHICAGO & LONDON

CHARLES R. WALGREEN FOUNDATION LECTURES

THE UNIVERSITY OF CHICAGO PRESS, CHICAGO & LONDON
The University of Toronto Press, Toronto 5, Canada

Foreword

A moral approach to the subject of democracy may not seem unusual to most people, but to many political scientists it will appear naïve or novel or unrealistically antique. The political scientist who emphasizes the *science* in his profession or who thinks of his subject as "morally neutral" will find Professor Hallowell's treatment challenging. The resurgence, however, of the realists, the traditionalists, the Aristotelians, or the neo-scholastics—whatever name they choose to be known by—brings to the fore the ancient conviction that morals, in the sense of the choice of the right means (characterized by the virtue of prudence) to rationally determined objective ends, lie at the very foundation of politics.

Professor Hallowell's contributions in this field have been outstanding, and the present work, based upon his Walgreen Foundation lectures, is offered for the better understanding of his school of thought.

JEROME G. KERWIN, *Chairman*

Charles R. Walgreen Foundation for the Study of American Institutions

Acknowledgments

With some minor revisions, this book consists of six lectures which were given at the University of Chicago in the spring of 1952 under the auspices of the Charles R. Walgreen Foundation for the Study of American Institutions. And I should like to take this opportunity to thank the Foundation and especially its chairman, Professor Jerome G. Kerwin, for the encouragement it has given me in extending this invitation.

My colleagues at Duke have been most helpful in their criticism, and I want especially to thank Professors Robert R. Wilson, R. Taylor Cole, and Waldo Beach for the careful reading which they gave my manuscript. Miss Mary Evelyn Blagg has given me much helpful assistance in preparing the lectures for publication.

The following publications have kindly given me permission to use material which had been previously published: *Ethics*, *Theology Today*, and *Commonweal*.

JOHN H. HALLOWELL

DURHAM, NORTH CAROLINA
October 25, 1953

Table of Contents

I. Democracy—Fact or Fiction?

"Who is this new god called Universal Suffrage?" Pareto asked at the beginning of this century. And he answered: "He is no more exactly definable, no less shrouded in mystery, no less beyond the pale of reality, than the hosts of other divinities; nor are there fewer or less patent contradictions in his theology than in theirs. Worshippers of Universal Suffrage are not led by their god. It is they who lead him—and by the nose, determining the forms in which he must manifest himself. Oftentimes proclaiming the sanctity of 'majority rule,' they resist 'majority rule' by obstructionist tactics, even though they form but small minorities, and burning incense to the Goddess Reason, they in no wise disdain, in certain cases, alliances with Chicanery, Fraud, and Corruption."[1] Whatever the form of government, by whatever name it is called, it is always, according to the Italian sociologist, rule by some elite, a minority that rules either by deception or by violence. And many intellectuals today would agree with that judgment. Any view which regards democracy as having roots in objective reality is discarded as hopelessly naïve, a form of self-deception from which the student of politics should seek emancipation.

Pareto's pronouncement on the delusive character of political philosophy in general and of democratic political theory in particular is all the more impressive because it is proclaimed to be

---

1. Vilfredo Pareto, *The Mind and Society* (4 vols.; New York, 1935), Vol. IV, par. 2183. Quotations used with the permission of Harcourt, Brace and Co.

a *scientific* judgment. For it was Pareto's claim that his *Trattato di sociologia generale* (1915–16) was simply a scientific description of social reality and, as a consequence, that it was free from all metaphysical speculation, moral evaluations, and a priori principles. Explaining human motivation in terms of six principal types of "residues" which are conceived as being something more complex than what had earlier been called "instincts," Pareto, like many contemporary intellectuals, is impressed with the essential irrationality of human behavior. All political philosophies, systems of ethics, theologies, and metaphysical theories, according to Pareto, are simply verbal manifestations of dominant residues. All can be subsumed under the one classification "derivation."[2] A derivation, he argued, is not accepted because it is true or rejected because it is false but is accepted if it corresponds to our residues and rejected if it does not. Only the scientific method, what Pareto calls the "logico-experimental" method, yields truth; only scientific theories are rational. Theories of progress, democracy, justice, nationalism, internationalism, or socialism are all non-logical derivations. A belief in "natural rights," in "justice," or in "law" is a kind of superstition or prejudice. None of them is a scientific concept, and hence none of them is rationally derived, rationally defensible, true or false. But, in any case, derivations are not very important in determining social change, for it is not by ideas that men are motivated, but by their residues. Says Pareto:

Theologians, metaphysicists, philosophers, theorists of politics, law, and ethics, do not ordinarily accept the order indicated. They are

2. According to Pareto: "Concrete theories in social connections are made up of residues and derivations. The residues are manifestations of sentiments. The derivations comprise logical reasonings, unsound reasonings, and manifestations of sentiments used for purposes of derivation: they are manifestations of the human being's hunger for thinking. If that hunger were satisfied by logico-experimental [i.e., empirical-scientific] reasonings only, there would be no derivations; instead of them we should get logico-experimental theories. But the human hunger for thinking is satisfied in any number of

inclined to assign first place to derivations. What we call residues are in their eyes axioms or dogmas, and the purpose is just the conclusion of a logical reasoning. But since they are not as a rule in any agreement on the derivation, they argue about it till they are blue in the face and think that they can change social conditions by proving a derivation fallacious. That is all an illusion on their part. They fail to realize that their hagglings never reach the majority of men, who could not make head nor tail to them anyhow, and who in fact disregard them save as articles of faith to which assent is deference to certain residues.[3]

All philosophical discourse, political debate, attempts at ethical evaluation, are forms of "haggling," a futile exercise of the vocal chords or a mere scribbling of the pen. For it is not by reason that the destiny of men is determined but by deception, fraud, and force. Government, whatever the name applied to it for propaganda purposes, is always rule by the few in their own interest. Indeed, Pareto tells us, "the art of government lies in finding ways to take advantage of . . . sentiments, not in wasting one's energies in futile efforts to destroy them. . . . The person who is able to free himself from the blind dominion of his own sentiments is capable of utilizing the sentiments of other people for his own ends."[4]

And all this is proclaimed as a new insight into government, an insight made possible by the development of that new science of society called "sociology." But as a matter of fact, Thrasymachus anticipated it in the fourth century B.C., and Machiavelli expressed somewhat similar sentiments with respect to the art of government in the sixteenth. What Pareto has done is simply to restate the ancient Sophistic argument under the guise of scientific research. As Professor Melvin Rader has pointed out:

The advantage of Pareto's book is that it not only suggests ruthless tactics, but offers a clever defense against the pangs of conscience.

---

ways; by pseudo-experimental reasonings, by words that stir the sentiments, by fatuous, inconclusive 'talk.' So derivations come into being" (*ibid.,* Vol. III, par. 1401).

3. *Ibid.,* Vol. III, par. 1415.   4. *Ibid.,* Vol. III, par. 1843.

It enlists the prestige of science in support of the will-to-power. As an apostle of the "logico-experimental method," Pareto bedecks his pages with algebraic signs and graphs, most of which are employed to excellent purpose. He "proves" his view that values are purely sentimental by marshaling a large amount of "inductive evidence." He thus appears to be a resolute defender of science, intent upon keeping "theory" uncontaminated by "practice" and "sentiment."

Since he adopts the role of a scientific purist, the casual reader is apt to misunderstand the import of his argument. His treatise in effect is an attack upon the life of reason, and this is true despite his apparent attachment to strict scientific method. As a matter of fact, he so unduly restricts the field of science that a great portion of existence is turned over to violence and passion.[5]

I

But Pareto is by no means alone in seeking to dress his cynicism up in the garments of "scientific objectivity." What Pareto called "derivations," Marx described as "ideologies," Sorel called "myths," and Freud labeled "rationalizations." There are important differences between these terms, and they are not to be equated, but Pareto, Marx, Sorel, and Freud are all agreed that men are motivated more by irrational considerations than by rational ones. But that they should concede that men do, in fact, feel some necessity for explaining their behavior in rational terms, for justifying themselves, says a great deal more about the rationality and ethical sensibilities of human nature than they intend to concede. For why should men feel any necessity at all for "rationalizing" their behavior, for providing "good" reasons for "real" ones, if, in fact, they are *essentially* irrational and controlled by forces, sentiments, or drives over which they have no rational control? How is it *possible* for them to do so?

And why is the social scientist exempt from the irrational forces that determine the thought and conduct of other individuals? On what grounds? If he is not exempt, of what value is his "science"?

5. *No Compromise: The Conflict between Two Worlds* (New York, 1939), p. 50. Quoted with the permission of the Macmillan Company.

On what grounds, for example, is Pareto's theory exempted from the designation which he applies to other people's theories? Is not his social theory but another example of a derivation?

No, he would probably reply, because his is a scientific theory and other people's theories are not. But Marx claimed that his theory was a scientific one, and so did Freud. The concept of the class struggle is, for Marx, a scientific concept just as the conception of libido is a scientific concept for Freud. Since both Marx and Freud explain things quite differently from each other and Pareto's theory differs from each of theirs, which science shall we listen to? What standard shall we use to choose between them? It cannot be the standard of scientific method, since each claims to have employed that method in reaching his conclusions. Which theory is a "derivation," and which is not? Which is an "ideology," and which is not? Which is "rationalization," and which is not?

"We may in fact state it as a rule," C. S. Lewis has pointed out, "that *no thought is valid if it can be fully explained as the result of irrational causes*." And it is a rule we apply every day of our lives. If a sober man tells us that his house is full of snakes, we may go with him to look for them; but if we know that he frequently suffers from delirium tremens, we pay no attention to him and dismiss his statement as a delusion. In our ordinary dealings with men we discount any beliefs that we even suspect have an irrational cause.

The same writer continues:

Now it would clearly be preposterous to apply this rule to each particular thought as we come to it and yet not to apply it to all thoughts taken collectively, that is, to human reason as a whole. Each particular thought is valueless if it is the result of irrational causes. Obviously, then, the whole process of human thought, what we call Reason, is equally valueless if it is the result of irrational causes. Hence every theory of the universe which makes the human mind a result of irrational causes is inadmissible, for it would be a proof that there are no such things as proofs. Which is nonsense.

But Naturalism, as commonly held, is precisely a theory of this sort. The mind, like every other particular thing or event, is supposed to be simply the product of the Total System. It is supposed to be that and nothing more, to have no power whatever of "going on of its own accord." And the Total System is not supposed to be rational. All thoughts whatever are therefore the results of irrational causes, and nothing more than that. The finest piece of scientific reasoning is caused in just the same irrational way as the thoughts a man has because a bit of bone is pressing on his brain. If we continue to apply our Rule, both are equally valueless. And if we stop applying our Rule we are no better off. For then the Naturalist will have to admit that thoughts produced by lunacy or alcohol or by the mere wish to disbelieve in Naturalism are just as valid as his own thoughts. What is sauce for the goose is sauce for the gander. The Naturalist cannot condemn other people's thoughts because they have irrational causes and continue to believe his own which have (if Naturalism is true) equally irrational causes.[6]

The intellectual who, like Pareto, denies the essential rationality of man and of the universe he inhabits involves himself in a contradiction from which he cannot rescue himself. But, wholly aside from the philosophical difficulties, what are the practical consequences? We may subscribe to that revolt against reason which expresses itself in terms of the overwhelming importance of economic factors in the determination of human behavior, or we may prefer the revolt against reason which ascribes overwhelming importance to the libido or the dominant residues; but

6. C. S. Lewis, *Miracles* (New York, 1947), p. 28. "By trusting to argument at all," Lewis points out, "you have assumed the point at issue. All arguments about the validity of thought make a tacit, and illegitimate, exception in favour of the bit of thought you are doing at that moment. . . . Thus the Freudian proves that all thoughts are merely due to complexes except the thoughts which constitute this proof itself. The Marxist proves that all thoughts result from class conditioning—except the thought he is thinking while he says this. It is therefore always impossible to begin with any other data whatever and from them to find out whether thought is valid. You must do exactly the opposite—must begin by admitting the self-evidence of logical thought and then believe all other things only in so far as they agree with that" (*ibid.*, p. 30). Copyrighted 1947 by the Macmillan Company and used with the Macmillan Company's permission.

we have opened the door for assertions that truth is simply a manifestation of nationalistic, racial, or class interests. If the art of government consists, as Pareto says it does, in finding ways to use other people's sentiments for one's own ends, then the totalitarian dictatorships of modern times would appear to represent the art of government at its best and most efficient. And if that is true, it is but a futile gesture to oppose them, and we had best now succumb to the inevitable. If justice, natural law, and natural rights refer to no objective reality, if democracy is but a word, then these words can be used in any fashion anyone wants to use them, and there is no way in which we can challenge his right to do so. If a Hitler or a Stalin claims that his system of government represents the purest democracy the world has ever known, that it is the perfect embodiment of justice, there is no way in which we can prove him wrong. We can say, of course, that we do not like what men like Stalin and Hitler do, but we cannot prove them wrong in doing what they do, nor can we defend by reason our preference for a different system.

II

The view that democracy is a fiction, at best a useful symbol, has found expression not only in the writings of Europeans like Pareto but in the writings of many Americans. And it has found, among others, explicit expression in the writings of Thurman Arnold, particularly in his *Symbols of Government* (1935) and *The Folklore of Capitalism* (1937).

The basic cause of our political confusion in America, he says, arises from a naïve faith in the existence of the "thinking man." The "thinking man" of the popular mythology is the man who is able to discern right principles and to prefer them to false ones. The "thinking man" is the man who is able both to discriminate and to act upon the basis of sound reason.

No competent psychologist, Arnold says, believes in the thinking man. He knows that such a man does not exist. But the trouble is that there are still too many people in the United States who do not take the psychologist's pronouncements on the nature of man seriously. They still insist that appeals in politics should be rational. They insist upon arguing the relative merits of communism, fascism, capitalism, and democracy. They are still naïve enough, Arnold says, to believe that something important and meaningful can emerge from that kind of argument. This illusion is fostered by educational institutions and by professors who have a professional interest in maintaining it. The trouble with "respectable people" generally is that they have faith in principles rather than in organizations. They are so intent upon principles, Arnold declares, that they do not even know how organizations really work.

Arnold points out that "in advertising the 'thinking man' has gone so completely that a modern advertising agency would be amazed at the suggestion that the best way to sell goods is by making a rational appeal." But he notes with regret that "in government the concept still reigns supreme. Men are still asked to diagnose the ills of social organization through the darkened lens of 'schools' of legal or economic theory. They still worry about choosing a 'system' of government."[7] But fortunately there are some "fact-minded persons who do not believe in the 'thinking man' and who do not expect to gain political objectives by making rational appeals."[8] These are the politicians, and they are to be distinguished from political scientists, who are "the high priests" of the mythology of the thinking man.

Only when we give up the illusion of the thinking man, stop arguing about such abstractions as capitalism, fascism, socialism, and democracy, stop expecting politicians to make rational appeals and to behave rationally, can we really begin, says Arnold,

7. Thurman Arnold, *The Folklore of Capitalism* (New Haven, 1937), p. 59. Quotations from this book are with the permission of the Yale University Press.

8. *Ibid.*, p. 60.

to solve our problems. Only when government becomes as en-
lightened as the modern advertising agency and frees itself from
all rational scruples, can government really do the work for which
it is designed.

To believe in the objective reality of law, justice, and rights,
Arnold thinks, is infantile. If we are to be "realistic" in dealing
with political problems, we must "grow up," give up our childish
ways of thinking, think and act like adults. But Arnold confesses
that "what a truly adult human race would be like the writer
cannot imagine."[9] He quotes with apparent approval, however,
another writer who describes the adult personality in this way:
"And now, when you have ceased to care for adventure, when
you have forgotten romance, when the only things worth while
to you are prestige and income, then you have grown up, then
you have become an adult."[10] But if "the only things worth while
to you are prestige and income," it would not appear to matter
very much under which system of government you live so long
as you can gain a position of prestige within it and enjoy a reasonably comfortable standard of living. If, moreover, prestige and
income are "the only things worth while," it would appear that
the means employed to acquire them are of little importance. If
it involves suffering for others, what some would call "injustice,"
we can always ease our conscience (for our conscience has a way
of intruding itself) by repeating over and over to ourselves that
justice is simply a word and no one knows what it means anyway.
And if the conflict between our desire for prestige and income
and the voice of conscience becomes too great to bear, we can
always turn to some psychiatrist who will assure us that the voice
of conscience is a vestige of infantilism. He will reassure us and
send us happily on our way.

Lest I seem to assign to the psychiatrist too large a role in
Arnold's scheme of things, let it be pointed out that he himself
assigns to the psychiatrist a major role in that system of govern-

9. *Ibid.*, p. 163.   10. *Ibid.*

ment that will dispense with the illusion of the thinking man. In a book entitled the *Symbols of Government*, Arnold summarizes what he calls "a philosophy for humanitarian politicians" in these words:

From a humanitarian point of view the best government is that which we find in an insane asylum. In such a government the physicians in charge do not separate the ideas of the insane into any separate sciences such as law, economics, and sociology; nor then instruct the insane in the intricacies of these three sciences. Nor do they argue with the insane as to the soundness or unsoundness of their ideas. Their aim is to make the inmates of the asylum as comfortable as possible, regardless of their respective moral deserts. In this they are limited only by the facilities of the institution. It is, of course, theoretically possible to treat the various ideas and taboos which affect modern society, just as the alienist treats the delusions of his patients as factors which condition their behavior. This precludes any classification into sound or unsound theories. . . . The advantages of such a theory for purposes of thinking about government are that we escape the troublesome assumption that the human race is rational. We need not condemn policies which contradict each other solely on the ground that the action of government must be logically consistent. . . . The theory eliminates from our thinking the moral ideals which hamper us wherever a governmental institution takes practical action. . . . It frees us from the necessity of worrying about names, and arguing about the respective merits of communism, fascism, or capitalism—arguments which have. the unfortunate effect of creating phobias against practical and humanitarian measures.[11]

Arnold lists a number of other advantages that flow from the concept of government as an insane asylum, but these are the principal ones.

Most of us, I think, would not describe the organization of an insane asylum as a government, let alone the best government, for we think of government as an organization of responsible individuals and insane persons are clearly not responsible persons. If we were forced to use a political label to describe the ad-

11. Thurman Arnold, *Symbols of Government* (New Haven, 1935), pp. 232 ff. Quoted with permission of the Yale University Press.

ministrative organization of an insane asylum, we would, I thi describe it as a benevolent despotism. Arnold apparently belie that only when we learn to regard the mass of citizens as patients in need of psychiatric therapy can we make real progress toward the solution of our social and economic problems. Many difficulties with his view suggest themselves, but one in particular emerges prominently. How are we to distinguish the social psychiatrists from the citizen-patients? Who are to be the patients, and who are to be the custodians? And if reason is of no avail in distinguishing sound principles from unsound ones or true theories from false ones, by what standard are we to separate the mass of the insane population from the sane minority? Presumably those who call themselves psychiatrists will have the first claim on sanity. The rest of us must patiently submit to being made as comfortable as possible.

George Orwell has described the horror of such a system in a way that should leave a lasting impression upon anyone who has read his *Nineteen Eighty-four*. C. S. Lewis has depicted the same horror with even more profound insight into the demonic forces behind it in *That Hideous Strength*. I wish that it were possible to dismiss Arnold's suggestion with the hearty laugh that it deserves; but, unfortunately, there is a sense in which the world is becoming as mad as Arnold thinks it is already, and we have witnessed the rise of political regimes in which the concept of government as an insane asylum is rapidly being realized. Unless we recover our capacity to distinguish truth from falsehood, goodness from evil, beauty from ugliness—unless we recover, above all, our sense of humor that is founded upon the rationality of man—there is grave danger that we, too, shall succumb to the horror that is held out to us as the promise of being made as comfortable as possible.

Arnold sees no essential difference between communism, fascism, and so-called "capitalistic democracy." They are all engaged in the same activities, albeit rationalized differently, and with the exception that some are more cruel than others. "In Russia, Germany, and Italy, where old ideals were suddenly swept away," he wrote in 1937, "a certain necessary realism has compelled these governments to recognize that the political party is always the real government. They therefore dragged political machinery out into the open and made the political leader the nominal as well as the actual governor. This enabled them to use political techniques more frankly and openly."[12] If I understand him correctly, Arnold is saying that the dictatorships have the virtue of doing frankly and openly what our parties must do deceitfully and less openly. Our political system will reach maturity, he suggests, when we can build a political organization in America that can operate with equal frankness. In Germany, Russia, and Italy, he says, "trials became an admitted method of political propaganda," while "in this country the trial of political issues by the Supreme Court of the United States, while it was actually political propaganda, was supposed to be something else."[13]

Although Arnold admires the frankness with which the Fascist and Communist regimes can employ political techniques "realistically," he is sincerely disturbed by the cruelty in which the employment of those techniques frequently results. After quoting a panegyric on the Russian regime by Walter Duranty, in which Duranty declared that Joseph Stalin is "making men out of mice, and putting courage, backbone and unity into a people that have been slaves for centuries,"[14] Arnold says that after Stalin abandoned the technique of great dramatic spectacles "for a great purge, the morale and prestige of Russia fell."[15] And Arnold is frankly perplexed. "International opinion realized," he wrote, "that Russia, for some inexplicable reason, was failing in organizational methods, in spite of the evidence of the internal power which such a purge represented."[16] What he fails to understand

---

12. *Folklore of Capitalism,* p. 344.
13. *Ibid.*
14. *Ibid.,* p. 345.
15. *Ibid.,* p. 346.
16. *Ibid.*

is the fact that purges and persecutions, cruelty and bloodshed, torture and concentration camps, are *essential* features of the "realistic" political techniques employed by the totalitarian dictatorships. The great Russian purges of the 1930's were not the first purges under the dictatorship of the Communist party, nor were they the last. They were only the most public and the most dramatic. For one who boasts of his realism, Arnold is exceedingly naïve when he speaks of the "internal power" revealed by such purges and when he expresses genuine surprise at their occurrence.

Perhaps he would not have been so surprised and shocked, had he remembered one of the principles he enunciates at the conclusion of his book. "The ceremonies which an institution adopts to reconcile its conflicting ideals," he wrote there, "are addressed to its own members, not to outsiders. Therefore they are seldom convincing to the critics of the institution."[17] He illustrates this principle by the following example:

> The persecution of Jews in Germany as a means of building morale is almost incomprehensible to an outsider. An outsider who judges this kind of ceremony by his own standards is therefore very easily misled into thinking that an institution which does such queer or such immoral things cannot endure. . . . The only realistic way to judge the effectiveness of any ceremony is to observe its effect on the institution itself, not on those outside of it. If the ceremony increases confidence and quiets doubters, the fact that it is illogical and absurd is immaterial.[18]

Now it is clearly inconsistent for Arnold to be shocked at the Fascist and Communist purges and persecutions when his own principles of what he calls "political dynamics" suggest that they are necessarily incomprehensible to "outsiders" and are sometimes necessary to "increase confidence and quiet doubters." It might be pointed out, incidentally, that some people on the "inside" find these practices just as incomprehensible and shocking

17. *Ibid.,* p. 358.   18. *Ibid.,* pp. 358–59.

as do many on the outside, and none, perhaps, more acutely than the victims themselves.

Arnold is not only genuinely disturbed by the cruelty of the methods employed by Hitler and Stalin but by their crudity. He does not think that such methods would be employed if the reins of government were held by what he frequently refers to as "respectable people." Instead of the lash and the torture rack, "respectable people" presumably would resort to the more refined and subtle methods of psychoanalysis, resorting only in extreme cases to the electric-shock treatment or the severance of the frontal lobes of the brain. But that these more "scientific" methods would prove less cruel and crude when used by "respectable people" unrestrained by any rational or moral considerations seems hardly likely.

It is not programs and principles that should concern us, Arnold insists, but the character of the men who control our organizations. All we need "to worry about is the character of the people who are gradually coming into power." Are they "good organizers and at the same time tolerant and humanitarian?"[19] But how are we to know whether they are good men if we cannot examine and rationally evaluate the principles that motivate them and the programs which they advocate? Arnold provides us with no standard of good character—indeed, denies that goodness has any objective meaning, yet insists that it is good men, and good men alone, who are going to solve our problems. He cannot maintain at one and the same time that all ethical judgments are nonsense and resort to an ethical judgment as the bulwark of his theory. Not only does Arnold neglect to provide objective criteria in terms of which we may distinguish "good men," but he also neglects to consider how the use of certain political techniques may corrupt those who employ them. It is not inconceivable that some of the Nazi and Communist leaders were once "respectable people" animated by humanitarian motives. The

19. *Ibid.,* p. 342.

literature of Communist disillusionment amply records the moral deterioration that gradually takes place in one who subordinates loyalty to principles to loyalty to an organization. But it is precisely this subordination that Arnold specifically and consistently advocates. Certainly we need organizations in order to implement our political principles; but to insist that it is meaningless, useless, and unnecessary to inquire into the truth or falsity, goodness or badness, of the principles embodied in organizations and that it is necessary only to be loyal to the organization is to become a slave. Why should I give my loyalty to one organization rather than to another? Should I remain loyal to an organization irrespective of what it does? These are not questions to which Arnold has any answer. He can explain in psychological terms, he thinks, why a person happens to be loyal to a particular organization at a particular time; but he has no basis for deciding whether a person *ought* to be loyal to that organization, whether it is good or bad for him and for society that he should be loyal.

Arnold is impressed with the wide discrepancy between political and economic ideals and political and economic practices. He is by no means the first to observe these discrepancies, but he does have a talent for describing them in an amusing way. And he is constantly torn between the ludicrous aspects of this discrepancy and the tragedy of it. His mood is a curious compound of bemused sophistication and serious alarm. He resists the mood of cynicism whenever it creeps over him and holds fast to a belief in the existence of humanitarian-minded men to pull him out of the slough of despond.

No one denies that there is often a wide discrepancy between professions of faith and actual practice, between principles and actions. The question is how we should interpret such discrepancies. The immature reaction is to say that if I cannot attain perfection, I will not even try; if practice can never be squared with principles, then principles are nonexistent. The mature man, on the other hand, learns to live with imperfection—in himself, in others, and in society—without making a standard of imperfection.

Arnold is especially concerned with capitalism, and he has amassed considerable evidence to show that the theory in terms of which capitalism is described and defended in twentieth-century America bears little resemblance to actual practice. He concludes that the vocabulary of capitalism is a kind of folklore or fiction. No one who seriously examines the evidence would dispute his contention that actual economic practices in America today are far removed from the nineteenth-century theory of capitalism. But it seems to me that he goes much further than is necessary when he then concludes that capitalism as a theory never found any real reflection in reality. One of the reasons why he is able to discern the present-day discrepancies between capitalistic theory and current capitalistic practice is because capitalism has a real meaning. Arnold has performed a genuine service when he draws our attention to the wide gap between our economic theory and our economic practice. But instead of suggesting that we should bring our practice more in line with our theory or suggesting an economic theory that would reflect our present-day economic aspirations better than the older capitalistic theory, he concludes that theory's only importance is as rationalization. Thus, it seems to me, he denies the possibility of ever finding solutions to our problems by rational means. But it is only in terms of reason that we can recognize problems as problems and do something about them. Experience has to be interpreted before it has any meaning, and the only instrument of interpretation we have is our rational capacity. It is one thing to point out, as Arnold does, that names often bear no real relationship to the thing they are supposed to describe, but it is quite another thing to deduce from this fact that names, therefore, *never* refer to any objective reality.

This confusion is reflected in Arnold's discussion of democracy. Democracy, he tells us, has changed in recent decades from a creed to a political fact. The "principles" of democracy, he says, were once worshiped as fundamental truths, and democracy was once regarded as a set of guiding principles. Now we know that democracy is simply "a name for a type of organization controlled by voters." And we have discovered that "it is immaterial whether democracy is morally beautiful or not." We are no longer troubled by the fact that political platforms are "inconsistent with political action." Politicians have learned to use the techniques of advertising, where slogans take the place of truth. They have learned how to take polls on public questions and thus ascertain the best way in which to frame their appeals. Principles and political platforms have become "more and more of a ceremony and less a matter of belief" to those who write them.[20]

All of this Arnold believes to be a highly desirable development and an improvement over former times, when people believed in the principles of democracy as fundamental truths. He describes it as a growth in "political realism" and implies that it represents a growth in maturity. He goes on to say that "this sort of political realism about democracy was brought home to us by the success of the dictatorships in Russia and Germany. In these countries the revolutionary governments undertook

20. *Ibid.*, pp. 40–41. "Today," says Arnold, "when sophisticated men speak of democracy as the only workable method of government, they mean that a government which does not carry its people along with it emotionally, which depends on force, is insecure. They mean that it is better for a government to do foolish things which can have popular support than wise things which arouse people against it. They mean that if a man is not contented, material comforts will do him no good. They mean that the art of government consists in the technique of achieving willing popular acceptance; that what people *ought* to want is immaterial; that democratic government consists only in giving them what they *do* want; that progress in government can come only by improving the *wants* of the people through the technique of removing their prejudices; and finally, that the removal of prejudice must come first or material and humanitarian progress, imposed by force, will fail" (*ibid.*, pp. 44–45).

deliberately to arouse the intense enthusiasm of their peoples and to keep it at a high pitch. The method used was not rational; it was the rhythm of uniforms, salutes, marching feet, and national games. The strength of Hitler lay in the fact that he put everyone to work and managed to develop national pride. His weakness lay in his persecutions." Immediately following this analysis of our political awakening, Arnold goes on to say:

Such persecutions are not, I believe, *necessary* to the exercise of national power or the development of national morale. The reason why they are apt to occur in times of change is that respectable people in such times are too devoted to principles to solve immediate problems or to build up morale by the objective use of ceremony. They are too obsessed with the principles of government by the people to know how it works. This principle that national morale is more important than logic and that the present is more important than the future is little understood in an age when people who should know how to rule are lost in a search for universal truth.[21]

Arnold overlooks the fact that persecution and terror are an essential part of the political techniques employed by totalitarian dictatorships. Because the Fascist regimes have no genuine political philosophy, because they are the embodiment of what Hermann Rauschning had aptly called the "revolution of nihilism," war and warlike activities must take the place of ideas. The Fascist regimes are able "to arouse intense enthusiasm . . . and to keep it at a high pitch" only by keeping the nation in a continuous revolutionary turmoil. Since they have no aspirations that can be satisfied, no program that can be realized, they can remain in power only by keeping the nation in a constant state of crisis; when no real crisis exists, crises must be invented. It is an attempt, as one writer has pointed out, to maintain a *permanent* state of revolution. "Opposition groups have to be seized, the party has to be regularly purged, trials and expulsions have to take place. All this means stamina to a dictatorship, and even

21. *Ibid.*, pp. 41–42.

the most peaceful work of daily life must show the touch of warlike activity. There are a thousand battles going on: the battle of grain, the battle for raw materials, the fight for joy after work, the battle of the birth rate. And they are all merely preparations for the supreme battle for world power."[22] The Jews have to be persecuted, tortured, and killed because they are depicted as the archenemy of the Aryan race; the kulaki must be liquidated because they stand in the way of the fulfilment of the proletarian revolution; and after the Jews and kulaki have vanished from society the party must be purged of counter-revolutionary elements. The terror, the persecution, the murder, can never stop, for it is the very thing upon which the dictatorships live. Without it they would die.

In 1934 one of the leaders of the British Union of Fascists declared:

Fascism is real insurrection—an insurrection of *feeling*—a mutiny of *men* against the conditions of the modern world. It is completely characteristic of this aspect of Fascism in its early stages, both in Italy and in Germany, that the movement should have grown to full strength without either logical theory behind it or cut-and-dried program in front of it. The men who built Fascism in Italy and Germany . . . leave theories to the intellectuals and programs to the democrats who have betrayed them with programs for a century. The Fascist . . . acts, in fact, instinctively, and not theoretically.[23]

Fascism is the practical manifestation of the repudiation of reason in the realm of politics. "The fascist scheme of things," according to Lawrence Dennis, "is an expression of human will which creates its own truths and values from day to day to suit its changing purposes."[24]

22. Sigmund Neumann, *Permanent Revolution* (New York, 1942), pp. 41–42. Quoted with the permission of Harper & Bros.

23. James Drennan, *B.U.F.: Oswald Mosely and British Fascism* (London, 1934), pp. 212–13.

24. *The Coming American Fascism* (New York, 1936), p. 105.

Arnold insists that political action is more important than political theory, that loyalty to organizations is to be preferred to loyalty to principles, that the function of public debate is ceremonial and symbolic only, and that there is no essential difference between the demagogue and the statesman.[25] At the conclusion of his book on the *Symbols of Government*, Arnold declared that it was his hope in writing the book that "a competent, practical, opportunistic government class may rise to power."[26] That such a class may well rise to power in the name of democracy, however, is no guaranty that its actions will be less brutal than those of the Fascists; for if democracy has no genuine creed, if it is based upon no rational principles, if it rests upon no fundamental truths, we shall have no standards of judgment left with which to evaluate its actions. Whatever such a class does will be democratic, and from those actions there will be no appeal. Arnold would probably reply that it is a characteristic of democracy that the rulers must achieve "willing popular acceptance" for their rule and that this alone would constitute an effective check upon their actions. But there are all kinds of ways of winning popular acceptance, as he knows; and the modern totalitarian dictatorships have shown how easy it is to manufacture consent, to generate enthusiasm, and to win mass approval. Much of what Hitler did was done with what certainly looked, from the outside at least, like "willing popular acceptance." Underlying Arnold's belief that the necessity of

25. "In other words," says Arnold, "every person seeking power over groups of people, without the use of physical force, must create enthusiasms which will make them follow him. There is no difference between the demagogue and the statesman, except on the basis of a judgment as to the desirability of the social ends and social values which move the one or the other. The man with the social values which you do not like, you will call the demagogue. You will say that he appeals to emotion and not to reason. This, however, is only because 'reason' is the respectable end of the two polar terms, 'reason' versus 'emotion,' and you instinctively want it to point toward your own organization" (*Folklore of Capitalism*, p. 380).

26. *Symbols of Government*, p. 271.

winning popular acceptance constitutes the only necessary check upon government is the assumption that no people will ever want to do that which is contrary to their own best interests. Yet this is an assumption which would appear to have been proved false by recent political experience, if not by the more remote history of the human race. One of the things which distinguish the modern dictatorships from many of the dictatorships in the past lies precisely in the fact that the modern dictatorships arise as mass movements and exist on a broad base of popular approval. One of the reasons why democratic government must be constitutional government, as the framers of the American Constitution recognized, is the necessity for putting specific restraints upon will, whether it be the will of one, of a few, or of many. The *unbridled* rule of the majority, as John Adams and many of his contemporaries realized, leads straight toward mass tyranny. If democracy means nothing more than giving the majority of the people what they want, then it is practically indistinguishable from fascism.

If democracy is but a name that refers to no objective reality, if, in short, it is a fiction, then the struggle against tyranny is both meaningless and futile, and we had best now surrender to the inevitable. On the other hand, there is the possibility that there is a real difference between democracy and tyranny and that freedom is something more valuable and real than a name. However difficult it may be precisely to define democracy, to describe the principles that ought to animate it; however short we may fall in practice of the realization of those principles, it may still be worth while to continue the search and to try to improve the practice. We need not prove that democracy is perfectly realized in practice, in order to answer the argument that it is nothing but a fiction. There is a sense in which democracy is as much aspiration as it is fact; but that aspiration has certainly profoundly influenced our political and social institutions and made life in America something quite different from what it is in the Soviet Union or what it was like in Germany under the Nazis. This does not mean that we can be complacent with our achievement, that we should not strive to bring our democratic practice more in line with our democratic theory; but neither does it mean, on the other hand, that we should disparage the achievement we have made or despair of democracy because we can never perfectly realize its principles in practice.

Arnold's attitude—and he is by no means alone—appears to be one rather common among disillusioned liberals. If principles are imperfectly realized in practice, then principles are a snare and a delusion. They can seem to find no middle ground between an excessive optimism and an excessive pessimism; if they can no longer be idealists, they will be cynics. And the bitterness of their cynicism is often an indication of the profundity of their disillusionment.

But a man is often better than his philosophy. As a public servant and federal judge, Arnold's record is one of unselfish service to the common welfare. Although he disparages adherence to principles in the writings we have considered here, it is significant that he frequently acted in public life as one who was genuinely motivated by humanitarian principles. My concern here has not been with Arnold's record as a man or as a public servant but with Arnold as a political philosopher; and it is in this capacity that I have found him gravely deficient. The deficiency of his theory lies precisely in the fact that his theory disparages the very principles upon which his own career as a public servant has been based. It is unlikely that humanitarian sentiments are sufficient to sustain humanitarian action in politics, especially when those sentiments are not grounded in philosophical convictions. Without philosophical convictions, humanitarian sentiments are likely to evaporate in time of stress and strain. Sentiment alone is not enough.

Arnold's writings have been singled out here for analysis not because they are unique in the ideas which they express but rather because they are representative of a large segment of American intellectual thought. It has become increasingly fashionable, in intellectual circles at least, to insist that moral judgments are nothing more than expressions of individual taste or preference, that law is simply what certain men arbitrarily declare it to be, that ultimately only force alone can resolve the conflict between our "deep-seated preferences."[27] If it is an illusion to believe that there is a forum of reason and conscience to which we can submit our differences for judgment, then we have no alternative but to submit them by default to the arena of force. In that arena it is not the best reason that will prevail but the mightiest fist.

III

The dominant characteristic of the intellectual climate of our times, curiously enough, is an animus against everything intellectual. Never was the rationality of man subjected to a more sustained attack than it is today, and from all quarters, scientific, philosophical, and even theological. And this is a curious fact that we should be using the methods of science, philosophy, and theology to discredit the existence of the very thing upon which the validity of those methods depends, namely, the rationality of man and of the universe he inhabits.

That man is a rational being living in a rational universe will be the premise of my argument. And it is a premise, it seems to me, which anyone must accept if he is to argue for the truthfulness of anything. For what is the point of any intellectual discussion if it necessarily begins in irrationality and ends in irrationality? How can we hope to communicate anything meaningful to one another apart from a capacity for reasoning that is common to all? And what are we talking about if the concepts and words we use refer to no objective reality?

27. See my *Main Currents in Modern Political Thought* (New York, 1950), esp. chaps. x and xv.

The attempt of many intellectuals today to *prove* that man is essentially irrational is bound to be self-defeating; for, in the very process of assembling evidence for their contention and arguing in behalf of it, they concede, of necessity, a great deal more than they intend. For they can only hope to prove their case by using the very capacity they deny and by appealing to that capacity in others in order to win agreement. If man were essentially irrational, there would be no such thing as evidence, argument, or proof. Indeed, there would be no such concept as "irrationality." If the phrase "irrational behavior" means anything, it is because we have some understanding of what "rational behavior" means. We could have no concept or understanding of irrationality if we did not already have some understanding of rationality.

My argument will rest upon what might be called the principles of classical realism, principles that commend themselves to common sense. I am aware that there are philosophers who scorn the appeal to the common sense of men as naïve; yet the appeal to common sense, if it is not the ultimate standard of truthfulness, is not an appeal that can be ignored. Georg Simmel once facetiously remarked: "A philosopher is one who articulates what everybody else knows"; and, despite its intended humor, his remark points to a profound truth. We expect greater subtleties of thought of the philosopher than we expect of the man in the street; but if the philosopher's philosophy violates everything that appears to the man in the street as "common sense," we can be sure that there is something radically wrong with his thinking.

The principles of classical realism might be summarized in this way. There exists a meaningful reality whose existence does not depend upon our knowledge of it. Or, in more technical philosophical language, "The world is made up of contingent, substantial entities existing in an order of real relations, which is independent of human opinion and desire."[28] This principle rejects both materialism and idealism, insists that both ideas and matter are real and that one cannot be reduced to the other. The world in which we live is an orderly universe—a cosmos, not a chaos.

A second principle of classical realism is that man is endowed with a faculty which enables him, at least dimly, to grasp the meaning of this reality. In technical language: "The mind is existentially diverse from that which it knows but formally identical with it. Because of the existential diversity, knowing is a relation. Because of the formal unity, the relation is the unique intentional relation of identity."[29] Knowledge does not involve the making or constructing of anything, but rather the discovery of what already exists. It is this principle, as Professor Wild points out, that enables the physicist "to understand the properties of a vapor without being physically vaporized" and enables the geologist "to understand the nature of a rock without becoming petrified."[30]

A third principle is that being and goodness belong together. Through knowledge of what we are, we obtain knowledge of what we ought to do. To know what man is, is to know what he should be and do. The knowledge of what man should do in order to fulfil his human nature is embodied in what has traditionally been called the "law of nature" or the "moral law." This law, though requiring positive laws to meet changing circumstances, provides universally applicable principles in terms

28. John Wild, "The Present Relevance of Catholic Theology," in Edward D. Myers (ed.), *Christianity and Reason* (New York, 1951), p. 26. Quoted with permission of the Oxford University Press.

29. John Wild (ed.), *The Return to Reason* (Chicago, 1953), p. 360. Quoted with permission of the University of Chicago Press.

30. John Wild, in *Christianity and Reason*, pp. 26–27. For an excellent elementary introduction to classical realism see John Wild, *Introduction to Realistic Philosophy* (New York, 1948).

of which we can guide our individual and social life toward the perfection of that which is distinctively human. This principle denies that there is any natural opposition between individual good and the common good; the restraints that are necessary for the development of a good man are identical with the restraints that make life in society possible.

Although the contemporary revolt against reason is without precedent in terms of its universality, it is not without historical antecedents. For the intellectual issues that divide men today resemble those which divided the nominalists from the realists in the later Middle Ages and, even earlier, the Sophists from Plato and Aristotle. Philosophy itself was born of that initial conflict, and we may hope that it may be reborn out of the conflicts that engage us today.

II. Democracy as the Art of Compromise

Politics, many contemporary students of politics declare, is concerned with the conflict of power-seeking interest groups. And politics is the art of getting as much as you can by mediation and compromise for the interest group you represent. The public interest is defined, if defined at all, simply as anything and everything that can be secured by the mediation of conflicting claims for power. Compromise not only is a self-sufficient political ideal but, many insist, the distinguishing and essential characteristic of democracy as a form of government.

At a time when clarity and agreement as to the meaning of democracy are so vitally essential, it is appropriate that such a view should be examined with care. For if these individuals mean, as some explicitly declare, that truth, justice, and the common good are too ambiguous to serve as guideposts in the democratic solution of conflict, then such assertions can and should not go unchallenged. Those who urge this view upon us, in order, as they believe, to chart a safer middle course between the Scylla of tyranny and the Charybdis of anarchy, may cause us eventually to founder upon the shoals of cynicism and to succumb through moral anarchy and political paralysis to the tyranny they would have us avoid.

I

For the purpose of analyzing the self-sufficiency of compromise as the animating principle of democratic politics, I should like to analyze critically some of the writings of Professor T. V.

Smith, who represents this position perhaps better than anyone else.[1] In a manner reminiscent of the first Marquis of Halifax, who wore the epithet of "trimmer" as a badge of honor, Smith declares: "A sense of guilt incident to the practice of compromise is perhaps the worst inner enemy of the democratic way of life."[2] And with this as his theme, he endeavors to prove that compromise not only is a desirable practice in politics but the distinguishing principle of the democratic way of life.

The only alternative to compromise as the animating and self-sufficient principle of democratic politics which he can conceive is dictatorship in the manner of a Hitler or a Stalin. The dissenter, accordingly, is placed in the uncomfortable position of espousing tyranny. "The vices of our practicing politicians we must compare not with the virtues projected from the consciences of secluded individuals," Smith insists, but with "the vices of fanatics who have become dictators."[3] That the vices both of democratic politicians and of dictators might legitimately be subjected to the scrutiny of conscience, he denies. We are told to compare what are acknowledged to be evils and to cherish the lesser evil. But how, if conscience is denied a valid role in the determination of either virtue or vice, we are to recognize the lesser evil, we are not told. That the vices of democratic politicians, moreover, become less vicious by comparison with the vices of dictators does not necessarily follow.

Smith seems to argue that because compromises are inevitable,

1. I have consulted the following books and articles by T. V. Smith: *The Legislative Way of Life* (Chicago, 1940); *The Compromise Principle in Politics* ("Edmund J. James Lectures on Government: Second Series" [Urbana, 1941]); *The Democratic Tradition in America* (New York, 1941); "Compromise: Its Context and Limits," *Ethics*, Vol. LIII, No. 1 (1942); "Is Congress Any Good, Anyhow?" *New York Times Magazine*, October 18, 1942; and *Discipline for Democracy* (Chapel Hill, 1942). This chapter is reprinted with minor revisions from *Ethics*, LIV, No. 3, 157–73, with the permission of the University of Chicago Press.

2. *The Compromise Principle in Politics*, p. 29.   3. *Ibid.*, p. 36.

they are also desirable. Compromise, he says, "arises in the narrow context of social necessity and functions in the expanding context of individual growth and social progress. By transmuting the necessary into the desirable men of good will make some minimum freedom of their uttermost fate."[4] That every social situation requires some compromises is a truism that can readily be granted, but that the necessity of making compromises thereby renders the practice desirable in *every* instance does not logically follow.

Many things are inevitable that are not necessarily desirable. The inevitability of the existence of crime will never be an argument for its desirability nor for the toleration of criminals. Often it is necessary for us to defend our lives and institutions by force of arms, but it does not follow that war, therefore, is a desirable institution or that men of good will, by transmuting the necessary into the desirable, must or should acclaim war as an ideal of life. To say that every social situation inevitably demands compromises says nothing whatsoever about the necessity or desirability of *particular* compromises in *particular* situations.

That compromise, moreover, is a practice which leads inevitably to "individual growth and social progress" is to claim more for the practice than is logically or historically justified. Such a practice can lead, and has led, to individual degeneration and social decay. Whether progress or decay will result from the practice of compromise will depend upon the *kind* of compromises that are made, not upon the practice itself but upon the *substance* of the compromises that are made.

II

So fundamental does Smith regard the principle and practice of compromise that he would define politics itself simply as "the institutionalized art of compromise."[5] "Democracy means,

4. *Ibid.*, p. 31.
5. "Compromise: Its Context and Limits," *Ethics*, LIII, 2.

politically speaking," he declares, "the process of clearing collective conflicts through a legislature; and it means, socially speaking, the way of living life together without condescension. Combining these two meanings, we may say that the democratic way of life is kept sound at its core . . . by the legislative way of doing things."[6]

Now what is this legislative way of doing things? First of all, the legislature is a place where "all points of view can meet on equal terms and have it out."[7] And "since no one can adequately represent the opposing view, each must be allowed to state his own case, to represent his own cause."[8] For "legislators owe only deference to one another, but both duty and victory to constituents back home . . . nobody in the legislature owes much to anybody else there."[9] The legislature, then, according to Smith, is a place where the representatives of all the various interests in society meet to champion those interests and to get the most they can by mediation and compromise for those interests they represent.

It is significant that he subordinates, if he does not completely eliminate, the deliberative function of the legislature to its representative function. And he conceives of that representative function in a novel way. Traditionally, we have thought of a representative as representing not only his constituents but his constituency and of representing his constituents not as members of any particular interest group but as citizens with obligations to the national interest and the common good of all. The effect of Smith's emphasis upon the representative as a representative of particular interests, moreover, is to subordinate the reason of the legislator to his will. The product of the legislature must be regarded, then, as the product not of the best thought of the legislators but of the will of the stronger. Law becomes exclusively an expression of will, and its sole sanction the force be-

---

6. *The Legislative Way of Life*, pp. 1–2.   8. *Ibid.*, p. 14.
7. *Ibid.*, p. 15.   9. *Ibid.*, p. 4.

hind it. If the primary function of the legislator is to "represent his own cause" with only "deference" to his fellow-legislators but with "duty and victory to constituents back home," how can the legislature be anything but a field of combat ever ready to disintegrate into chaotic futility or into servile submission to the will of the stronger? It is unlikely that mutual "deference," particularly when it is undefined and without substantive content, would long restrain the stronger party.

Underlying the democratic and legislative way of doing things, Smith declares, are certain fundamental assumptions. According to him, "before the legislature can function at all," (1) "we must assume that all major interests in a given society are equally legitimate"; (2) "we must assume that representatives of the great legitimate interests are equally honest"; and (3) "we must assume . . . that ideals (justice, for example) cannot be invoked to settle issues that involve quarrels as to what the ideals are or as to who owns them."[10] Let us analyze the implications of these fundamental assumptions.

Is it true that all major interests in a given society are equally legitimate? Is it possible to answer such a question categorically? Logically, the answer would appear to depend upon what the major interests propose; conceivably, their proposals may run the gamut from complete illegitimacy to complete legitimacy. In point of time, too, it is conceivable that a major interest might make proposals now that are illegitimate but which, if made at a different time under other circumstances, might be quite legitimate. Only by assuming beforehand, as Smith does, that the proposals of the major interests are *always* and in *every* situation legitimate, can one avoid the difficulty of providing (as he does not) some standard by which to measure degrees of legitimacy or, as a matter of fact, legitimacy itself. Since he does not provide such a standard, there would appear to be no logical reason for his introducing the concept of legitimacy at all. For,

10. *Ibid.*, p. 26.

if all major interests are *always* legitimate, they can never be illegitimate. When Smith speaks of the equal legitimacy of all major interests in a given society, then he simply means that the *test* of legitimacy can never be applied to any of their proposals in any given situation or at any time.

Now it is possible to conceive of a situation in which the fulfilment of one group's interest demands that another group yield its interests completely. If two interests are diametrically opposed and one can be realized only by making the realization of the other impossible, the technique of compromise does not contain in itself any principle by means of which it can be decided which interest is to prevail or what must be given up. That such situations are not only conceivable but do actually occur renders the assumption of the equal legitimacy of all major interests false—if legitimacy has any meaning at all.

In effect, Smith is saying that no proposal of any major interest can ever be subjected to the *test* of legitimacy. And that means that *whatever* any major interest proposes (i.e., regards as necessary for the realization of its equally legitimate interest) can never be condemned or turned down on the grounds that it is harmful to another interest, to society as a whole, or contrary to the principles of justice.

In practical terms it means that no proposal made by labor unions, business management, farmers, veterans, or any other major interest group can ever be rejected on the grounds that it is unreasonable, unwise, or unjust. Legislators must simply compromise whatever conflicts arise (but on what principles it is not clear) and assume, apparently, that what results is the most reasonable, wise, and just policy that can practically be achieved. That that is exactly how they often do proceed is no argument for the desirability of the procedure.

If all proposals made by major interests are assumed before they are made to be equally legitimate, if the content of proposals has nothing to do with their legitimacy, if there are no degrees of legitimacy, then in the last analysis the substance of the "compromise" effected must depend solely upon the relative strength of the opposing groups. Such a doctrine would appear to reduce politics (and democracy in Smith's terms) to domestic warfare.[11]

The second assumption underlying the democratic and legislative way of doing things, according to Smith, is that we must regard all the representatives of the major interests as being equally honest. The question that immediately occurs is: Why? What evidence is there for assuming that the representatives of all the major interests are or will be, in every situation and at every moment, equally honest? Is this not assuming more than is credible or justified by experience? The second assumption, like the first, claims too much, and it overlooks the fact that logically we can speak only of the honesty of particular men and that the honesty of these particular men depends upon what they do in particular situations and at particular times.

What are the practical consequences of accepting Smith's assumption with respect to the equal honesty of the representatives of all major interests? In effect, honesty is abandoned as a standard with which to measure the right of a person to represent a particular interest, as a standard with which to judge the truthfulness or sincerity of what he advocates, and as a standard with which to judge between rival representatives of the same interest or the representatives of different interests. If honesty is eliminated as a test of particular representatives, you have no choice but to give the same consideration to proposals made in the name of labor, let us say, by racketeers and genuine labor spokesmen. To which spokesmen are you to listen? With which representatives are you to make compromises? Apparently with those who find themselves in positions of the greatest power, whether honest or not.

If both the legitimacy of the demands and the honesty of the representatives have been eliminated as valid tests of either

11. Cf. Carl Schmitt, *Der Begriff des Politischen* (Hamburg, 1927).

the necessity or the substance of compromises, if power alone dictates the necessity of compromise and its content, how can such "compromises" be anything but temporary truces? What reason do we have to believe that any compromise will be kept any longer than is expedient, particularly when we eliminate any test of the honesty of the parties to the agreement? In all probability, the stronger party will not only dictate the substance of the compromise but demand, as time goes on and its position is strengthened, more and more concessions from the weaker party. What is to restrain the stronger party if you eliminate appeals to ideals—justice, for example?

For, according to T. V. Smith, one must assume, if a legislature is to function properly, that "ideals (justice, for example) cannot be invoked to settle issues that involve quarrels as to what the ideals are or as to who owns them." The question is: How is it *possible* to mediate differences, to make compromises, without some standard of justice, the public interest, and the common good? For the very nature of compromise presupposes some commonly acknowledged principles of justice in terms of which mutual concessions can be made. No one likes compromise for its own sake. We are willing to make compromises, when we do make them, because we value something more than we do the things we are giving up. Individuals will willingly give up some particular interest or claim only when interest in preserving something they regard as more important is greater. How can "compromises" which are dictated by the superior strength of one particular group or bloc be anything but the beginning of repeated demands by the stronger party for endless concessions from the weaker? If continued without any consideration of justice, the common good, or the public interest, such "compromises" might well end in the elimination of all compromise and eventually destroy the legislature itself— at least as a place of mediation, if not, perhaps, as an audience for the dictator.

If a compromise is to approximate a solution to conflict, it must be made within a framework of goals and values commonly shared and mutually respected by all parties to the agreement. If it is to approximate a solution, moreover, it must embody what is best in all proposals, what will best promote the common good; and this can be determined only by appealing to those purposes and values that are shared.

That there will be argument as to what constitutes the best means of promoting the common good, of realizing justice, is inevitable; but this is not necessarily, as Smith seems to imply, futile or deplorable. Much will depend upon the good will and honesty of the representatives, as well as upon their ability and willingness to engage in rational deliberation. The faith of democracy and of the legislative way of doing things is, essentially, a faith in the efficacy of argument, deliberation, and persuasion as the best means of arriving at the best possible policy. Such a faith assumes that argument will take place within a framework of principles and purposes which are commonly shared and that it will be dedicated to the purpose of distilling from assorted opinions those which are nearest to the truth and which most nearly embody the values to be preserved and promoted.

That discussion in democratic legislatures often is, in fact, unintelligent, bombastic, and carping does not disprove the fact that the faith of democracy demands a different kind of deliberation. It may mean that legislatures which engage in that kind of "discussion" are simply undermining and destroying the reason for their existence.

As a form of government, democracy rests upon the consent of the governed. Now real consent is a positive force arising out of inner conviction. It is not synonymous with passive acquiescence. It is found as the basis of government in greater proportion to constraint only in nations where there is a community of values and interests, where there is a positive affirmation of certain fundamental values common to the large majority of individuals and groups within the nation. It is, indeed, the existence of this affirmation of fundamental values which makes democratic, parliamentary government possible. A minority will agree to temporary rule by the majority, not simply because the minority cherishes the hope of someday becoming the majority, but because certain common interests transcend partisan interests. *The breakdown of democracy comes when this community of values and interests disintegrates, when common agreement on fundamental principles and purposes no longer exists, when partisans no longer endeavor to work through the state but to become the state.* Thus when Smith declares that "democracy does not require, or permit, agreement on fundamentals,"[12] he is proclaiming, in effect, the demise of democracy. If there is no agreement on fundamentals, there can be no discussion worthy of the name, no compromise that is anything but the extraction of endless concessions by force, no assurance that human rights will be respected—in short, nothing that cannot tomorrow turn into the most ruthless tyranny. And the ruthlessness and injustice of that tyranny will in no way be softened or made more tolerable by calling it "democracy."

III

Professor Smith acknowledges that there are limits to compromise; but on this point he does not appear to be entirely consistent. In one place he declares, for example, that "the limit of compromise is, beyond all doubt, not fixed primarily by appeal to conscience" and adds that "any conscience that thinks so becomes by that very fact an apologist for a covert form of dictatorship."[13] But, in another and more recent statement of his position, he insists that "a man is not a good man, who will compromise the core of himself, compromise, that is, the final principles by which he lives."[14] It is difficult, if not impossible,

12. *Discipline for Democracy*, p. 124.
13. "Compromise . . . ," *Ethics*, LIII, 4.
14. *Discipline for Democracy*, p. 128.

to reconcile these two statements, for if "a good man" will not "compromise . . . the final principles by which he lives," how is he to avoid doing so if he cannot legitimately appeal to his conscience (i.e., the final principles by which he lives) as a guide in deciding whether a particular compromise will require that he sacrifice these "final principles"?

He endeavors to reconcile the two points of view by saying that "conscience can remain supreme in its own house only if it admits its impotence in the field of collective action."[15] Or, as he explains it in more popular terms,

honest men cannot be direct parties to the sacrifice of principle, for that undermines the self-respect requisite to good citizenship. So we must have professional sacrificers of conscience—who themselves get sacrificed as "scapegoats" therefor—in order that the "best" citizens may make the compromises required by civilization and yet keep the self-respect which goes along with being civilized . . . politicians are the midwives to bring justice to birth through the painful process of compromising the consciences of honest men whose interests are in dispute.[16]

Or, as he puts it in still a third way, "the good man and the good citizen meet and merge in a society so peaceful that freedom of conviction is habitually permitted but never perpetrated"; and this, he adds, "is the end-goal of the democratic way of life."[17]

Smith so restricts freedom of conscience as to make it meaningless. How can you speak of a conscience that is free in every way except to act? It is mockery to speak of preserving freedom of conviction by restricting the legitimate jurisdiction of conscience to an individual's mind. What precisely does it mean to say that individuals are free to have convictions but not free to evaluate any actions or themselves to act (at least as it affects

15. *The Democratic Tradition in America*, p. 47.

16. "Is Congress Any Good, Anyhow?" *New York Times Magazine,* October 18, 1942.

17. *Discipline for Democracy*, p. 128.

others) in accordance with these convictions? In effect, Smith seems to be saying: Since a man is not a good man who will compromise the final principles by which he lives, he should delegate the task of making compromises to individuals who professionalize in the art (i.e., the politicians), who, if necessity requires, will sacrifice these final principles for him. How can a man remain a good man, in Smith's terms, and agree to such a procedure?

Smith would like to eliminate appeals to conscience and to ideals in politics because he is afraid that someone may try to impose "his" conscience or ideals on others. He is fearful of this, in the last analysis, because he does not believe that the content of conscience is the same for all men or that ideals are anything more than the rationalizations of subjective interests. Smith declares:

> Prematurity does not constitute finality, and moral certitude of the educated and sensitive falls short of certainty in the democratic way of life where "each counts for one and nobody for more than one." I must insist that the context in which compromise arises is such as to render suspect all claims of conscience to preferred consideration. . . . There is a little Hitler hidden in the bosom of every conscientious man as well as in the heart of the unconscientious; and the conscience that does not see itself as a power drive needing sublimation through politics is perhaps more dangerous to democracy than the conscience that crassly admits that it will have its way regardless.[18]

Accepting a perspective that is by no means uncommon today, Smith declares that anyone who talks about the dictates of conscience is simply trying to provide "good" reasons for "real" ones. He assumes that no real motives are ever genuinely good ones, and he recognizes no distinction between genuine and spurious justifications. He would recognize apparently no difference in the realm of religious ideals between a Thomas Aquinas or a Calvin and Aimee Semple McPherson; or in the realm of politics

18. "Compromise . . . ," *Ethics*, LIII, 4.

between a Lincoln and a Huey Long; or in political philosophy between Aristotle and Dr. Goebbels. The only differences he would apparently concede are that some are more subtle and involved than others.

"The realm of ideals open to man is diverse to the point of infinity," Smith declares[19] and implies that anything any individual declares to be an ideal is an ideal and that there is no rational way of preferring one to another. When the Nazis declare that world domination by the *Herrenvolk* is their ideal, or the Communists that a "classless society" to be achieved by a dictatorship of the proletariat and world-wide revolution is their ideal, or a democrat that the preservation of human dignity and freedom is his ideal, all you can say is that ideals "are diverse to the point of infinity" and that there is no accounting for the tastes of men.

Underlying Smith's assumption that there is no possible way of defining the content of conscience or rationally choosing between opposing ideals is the belief that there is no such thing as truth or right—at least in the realm of politics. It is a "superstition," Smith declares, that "truth is the only value which defines a civilization."[20] Truth is all-important only for scientists, whose exclusive business it is to conduct the search for it and then only for a truth which must always be tentative. "For science is the means—I shall suggest the *only* means—" Smith writes, "whereby truth is replenished."[21]

But science achieves meaning and can lay claim to truth only by transcending its own methods. The late Professor Alfred North Whitehead has demonstrated that without certain metaphysical presuppositions, which by their very nature cannot be empirically ascertained or proved, science could "explain" noth-

19. *The Democratic Tradition in America,* p. 50.

20. *Discipline for Democracy,* p. 39.

21. *Ibid.,* p. 23.

ing.[22] And by restricting truth only to whatever can be demonstrated, and then only tentatively, by the methods of science, Smith denies the attribution of truth to a whole body of experience that lies beyond the concepts and methods of science and further denies that anyone, excepting the scientist, has any obligation to seek, or means of recognizing, truth.

After ruling out appeals to conscience, Professor Smith declares that the limits to compromise consist of necessity, peace, and progress.[23] Smith nowhere defines progress; but it is difficult to see how he can have any conception of progress when he denies· the existence of any objective good in the realm of politics. Progress can have no objective meaning if there is no such thing as objective truth. And how can individuals possibly know whether they are making progress, whether a particular compromise will hasten or retard this progress, unless they can legitimately appeal to their conscience, i.e., to that knowledge they have of objective values and principles? Smith seems to be saying that we must assume that whatever results from compromise must be progress.

Compromise is also limited, Smith declares, by peace. "Since compromise is an alternative to war, it loses its nature if it does

22. See A. N. Whitehead, *Science and the Modern World* (New York, 1925). Another writer has pointed out that "to retain . . . the distinction of truth and falsity *even for science alone* we have to enlarge the scientific world and in enlarging it to modify it deeply, for what is added is not something of the same order but something different in kind, not having even an analogy with the rest. Knowing, the process that has to other events the unique relation of apprehending them, is above the causal order, in the sense that, although in it, it also knows it. Science as knowing transcends the scientific world; its claim to be true lifts it above the type of order its content depicts. Deny the claim and the content is worthless; admit the claim and the content is set in a larger context. Science can explain things naturally, but never itself. It cannot be true in a purely scientific world" (T. E. Jessop, "The Scientific Account of Man," in T. E. Jessop *et al.*, *The Christian Understanding of Man* [London, 1938], p. 40).

23. "Compromise . . . ," *Ethics*, LIII, 8 ff.

not lead to peace."[24] By "peace" he apparently means the absence of armed conflict. The absence of armed conflict may or may not be a good thing, depending upon what it implies. It is certainly not a good thing, even in Smith's own terms, if it means that individuals must sacrifice the final principles by which they live in order to achieve it.

And genuine peace is something more than the absence of armed conflict. It is a product of justice. Since we must necessarily take into account the *conditions* prerequisite to peace, we must necessarily examine the *substance* of compromises that are designed to bring about the conditions under which peace, as a positive fact, can be achieved. Only compromises that are made within a framework of common interests and values can approximate a solution to conflict and thus bring about the conditions prerequisite to genuine peace. Since Smith, however, denies that such a community of interests and values exists or is essential to the practice of compromise, he denies, in effect, the possibility of achieving peace by this technique. How can we know whether a compromise will lead to peace unless we can legitimately inquire into the goodness or badness of the content of particular compromises, into the relative legitimacy of conflicting proposals, and into the honesty and sincerity of those who are parties to the compromise?

Munich, Smith declares, was a bad compromise because it did not keep the peace.[25] We can condemn Munich not because of the things which were conceded but only because, in retrospect, we see that it did not succeed in avoiding armed conflict. Since he denies that we can legitimately subject the content of compromise to the scrutiny of reason and conscience, we can know whether a compromise, such as Munich, will keep the "peace" only after it has been made. Peace, therefore, as Smith uses the term, can constitute no limit to particular compromises because

24. *Ibid.*, p. 9.   25. *The Compromise Principle in Politics*, p. 43.

it is a standard of judgment which can be applied only *after* the compromise has been made.

If the absence of armed conflict, moreover, is regarded as the ultimate value and the ultimate standard of judgment, then nothing (not even the practice of compromise) is valuable because, if we consistently refuse to fight for anything, nothing is secure from destruction by tyrants. If men will not arm and fight against might for the preservation of principles they regard as more valuable than life itself, they have no choice but to surrender all principles to the will of the stronger and, indeed, as it usually turns out, their lives as well.

The third limitation to compromise which Smith recognizes is necessity. "Where compromise is not necessary," he says, "it can hardly be desirable,"[26] Since, as we saw earlier, Smith equates necessity with desirability, this statement would seem to mean no more than this: where compromise is not necessary (or read "desirable"), it can hardly be necessary (or read "desirable"). How, since necessity is defined in terms of itself, this constitutes a limit to compromise is inconceivable.

The limits Smith proposes—progress, peace, and necessity— when examined in the light of his basic assumptions, turn out to be no limits at all. Progress is equated with whatever results from compromise; peace constitutes no limit, because we can know whether a compromise will keep the peace only after we have made it; and necessity constitutes no limit, because it provides us with no standard with which to judge necessity except necessity itself.

IV

Why not give up compromising, Smith asks, "and return to the unequivocal conscience? But that is to accept dictatorship. To avoid dictatorship *somebody* must do compromising. It is a necessity for the democratic way of life, not to say for any

26. "Compromise . . . ," *Ethics*, LIII, 8.

form of social life. Then let the politician do it. He knows that game."[27] Elsewhere, Smith declares:

People . . . get killed in the conflicts of interest over which our politicians preside with vices short of crimes and with virtues not wholly akin to magnanimity. If in this process of accommodation, politicians sometimes lie, it is regrettable but it is better than dictatorship. If they sometimes truckle, it is despicable but better than dictatorship. If they are sometimes bribed, it is execrable, but better than dictatorship.[28]

Underlying these statements are three major assumptions, namely: (1) that conscientious individuals are incapable of making compromises; (2) that dictatorship is synonymous with the rule of conscience; and (3) that there is no alternative to dictatorship other than the acceptance with equanimity of politicians who sometimes lie, truckle, and "preside with vices short of crimes" over the conflicts of interest.

Let us examine the validity of these assumptions. If the politician described by Smith is capable, although unrestrained by conscience, of limiting his demands to what can be achieved by mediation, why attribute to the conscientious individual who recognizes substantive limits to his desires any less a capacity? "Con-science" means the shared or common knowledge of certain objective truths and values. There is no logical reason to suppose that because an individual believes that certain values transcend personal interests, he also believes that all individuals should be *coerced* into the acceptance of those values. If conscientious individuals resort to coercion, it is not their conscience that is at fault but something else. The conscientious individual, moreover, does not believe that he is the sole custodian of these truths and values or the final interpreter of their meaning. He does not claim, as Smith implies he claims, personal infallibility; but neither does his acknowledgment of fallibility render the values them-

27. *The Compromise Principle in Politics*, p. 38.

28. *Ibid.*, p. 36.

selves meaningless or nonexistent. The fact that no individual can know more than partial truth does not destroy the validity of the truth he does know and shares with others or render meaningless the final truth that can never be attained by anyone.[29] It is the cynics who contend that there is no truth where truth is incomplete who are most likely to become fanatics when their cynicism is no longer tolerable even to themselves.

Conscience does not automatically rule out all compromises, but only particular kinds of compromises. Because he knows *in advance* the limits of what may be safely conceded and knows what, ideally speaking, is the ultimate goal, it would appear that the perpetuation of the practice of compromise would be safer in the hands of the conscientious politician than in the hands of the politician unrestrained by conscience and limited only by judgments he may properly make after the compromise has been made. Mediation can be perpetuated only so long as it leads to the preservation of something the mediators regard as more important and more valuable than their particular interests. Compromise is good only if it enables us to realize goals that are shared, principles that are mutually respected, and embodies a good that transcends particular interests. The conscientious politician, the one who has some standard of truth and goodness, is likely to make better compromises than the politician who has no standard except the feeling that it is good to compromise.

That the rule of conscience is synonymous with dictatorship in the manner of a Hitler is a curious theory. For most students of government would agree, I think, that it has been the absence of any respect for truth, the denial of any objective values, the repudiation of principles, which are most characteristic of totalitarian dictatorships. The Fascist mentality, rather than reflecting

29. "A man may worship the trinity of truth, beauty and goodness, beholding them in all their uncompromised purity," Smith declares, "as long as he does not ask or permit other men to tell him what they mean and so water them down as to what both can agree upon" (*Discipline for Democracy*, p. 123).

the mentality of a conscientious person, is more like the mentality of a cynic. Despite its external appearance of order, tyranny is actually the manifestation of anarchy. Compulsion replaces consent in all spheres of life because there is no common agreement obliging consent in any sphere. Hitler was able to advance the claim of infallibility not because he was the most conscientious person in Germany, or because he was so regarded by the German people, but because the German people had abdicated all responsibility for deciding what is true and what is right. It was the prior repudiation of the dictates of conscience that made the rise of Hitler to political power a possibility.

Somewhat petulantly—and understandably so as a former congressman—Smith insists that "politicians are victims of generalized aggressions deflected from the nagging self-guilt of idealistic citizens," who refuse to participate in politics because it is too "dirty."[30] There is considerable truth in this observation; but the solution would appear to be not the elimination of conscientious considerations from politics but rather the conscientious assumption of civic responsibility by those who now ignore that responsibility. If politics is "dirty," it may very well be the fault of individuals who refuse to accept the responsibilities of citizenship, in which case, it ill behooves them, as Smith insists, to castigate the politicians they elect or allow to be elected. But that does not alter the fact that politics is often "dirty," nor does it justify the acceptance of "dirty politics" as the standard of what politics ought to be. Instead of insising that the conscientious assume the obligations which they cannot avoid as citizens of a democracy, Smith says, speaking of the politicians: "Let these moral middle men do this dirty work for you. They are paid to do it, and trained to do it."[31] Let them, he says, compromise your conscience for you while you look the other way; you can cherish your ideals in your privacy while politicians undermine

30. *The Compromise Principle in Politics*, p. 37.

31. "Compromise . . . ," *Ethics*, LIII, 13.

them in public. He does not add that if you do that very long, you are likely to find, as people in the totalitarian dictatorships have found, that there is scant solace, indeed, in ideals that can never be uttered or in a privacy that excludes even your own children.

The third assumption that Smith makes is that there is no alternative to dictatorship other than the acceptance with equanimity of politicians who sometimes lie, truckle, and "preside with vices short of crimes" over the conflicts of interest. One can certainly recognize the inevitability of imperfection in politics without making a standard of imperfection. That all men, including politicians, sometimes lie and engage in other vices short of crime does not mean that we have to accept our own or other men's imperfections with equanimity. And, certainly, the principles which democratic government aspires to realize will be placed in jeopardy if men make no effort to avoid lying and "presiding with vices short of crimes" over the conflicts of interest.

But democracy, Smith tells us, subscribes to no fundamental truths or principles, it is only a method. *"Democracy is whatever can be arrived at democratically,* and not another thing."[32] Any procedural restraint, divorced from all other considerations, cannot logically, however, impose substantive restraints and is no guaranty even of the continuation of the procedure itself. Suppose that a democratic legislature decided by democratic procedure to do away with civil liberties, suppose that it went further and decided by democratic procedure to do away with itself as a deliberative body—we would have no choice, if we accepted Smith's definition of democracy, but to accept this action as democratic. And this is something more than a moot point, for something very much like this has already happened in countries that were once democratic.

32. *The Democratic Tradition in America,* p. 15.

If a procedural way of doing things constitutes no limit to what is done, it is doubtful whether any procedure, as procedure, is a guaranty even of the procedure itself. Individuals will adhere to a particular procedure only so long as they recognize some good in it. And that good must, of necessity, be derived from something beyond the procedure itself. The existence of the possibility of mediation depends not only upon the availability of a mediating procedure but upon the willingness of individuals to subordinate their subjective interests to the common good. Without an affirmation of a community of values and interests, without the willingness to give up some particular interests in the interest of the common good, mediation is an impossibility.

Compromise as a *self-sufficient* principle divorced from considerations of truth and justice is simply, in the last analysis, the ancient Thrasymachian doctrine that might makes right. It is a doctrine born of despair and rooted in nihilism. If the faith of democracy is simply a belief in the principle of compromise for its own sake, it is a meager faith indeed, upon which to build in the future or to survive in the present.[33]

33. There is an excellent discussion of the role of compromise in politics by Oliver Martin in *Ethics*, LVIII (January, 1948), 118–22.

III. The Institutional Framework of Democracy

It is easier to describe the institutions of democracy than it is to define democracy in a succinct phrase or formula. As a form of government, democracy is best understood as comprising a whole complex of institutions all of which are essential to its functioning and no one of which may be isolated as its distinguishing characteristic. These institutions are designed individually and collectively to implement the principle that government should rest upon the consent of the governed. The idea of popular sovereignty has an ancient lineage, but it was not until modern times that we discovered the institutional means by which that idea might be more fully realized in practice. Because political power now resides in fact as well as in theory in the hands of the great mass of people, democracy is both the greatest opportunity the individual has ever had for determining his own political destiny and also the greatest responsibility. There is both gain and peril in the emergence of modern democratic institutions, and whether greater gain than peril depends upon how these institutions are conceived and utilized. Never has the individual had greater political freedom, but, by the same token, never has he had placed upon him greater responsibility. We have heard a great deal about the extension of freedom brought about by the development of democratic institutions, but we have heard less said than we should about the responsibilities which that extension of freedom carries with it.

No government is more easily susceptible to disintegration into anarchy than is democracy, and in no government does the choice between order and anarchy depend so largely upon the thoughts, actions, and decisions of individuals. If democracy fails, if it does disintegrate into anarchy, the fault lies clearly with the people themselves. This is their government; this is their opportunity and their responsibility.

I

Since democracy rests upon the principle that no government is legitimate which does not derive its powers and functions from the consent of the governed, democracy is, first of all, government by persuasion and deliberation. The government can exercise no power or perform any function to which the people have not given their consent. The people do not give their consent once and for all time, but the giving of consent is conceived as a continuous process. Consent is conceived, moreover, not as passive acquiescence but as active approval.

In order to insure that government will be founded upon the consent of the governed, that governmental policy will be a reflection of popular deliberation and decision, a number of institutions exist for that purpose. First of all, there is the whole range of civil liberties. There can be no real consent where there is no freedom of speech, of press, and of assembly. Individuals must be protected from arbitrary arrest and imprisonment, from the kind of legislative bills of attainder that were frequently used in the past to silence political opposition. Individuals must be free to present petitions to the government and to enumerate publicly their grievances. Individuals must feel secure in their persons, homes, papers, and effects against unreasonable and arbitrary searches and seizures. They must feel secure against the arbitrary taking of their life, liberty, or possessions. There must be an impartial judicial system to settle disputes in terms of the rule of law, and everyone should have equal access to these courts. The existence of these civil liberties does not insure that governmental policy will reflect popular deliberation, but such liberties are designed to provide an atmosphere of freedom in terms of which such deliberation can take place without fear of political reprisal. Too often we have taken the existence of such liberties for granted, and only the extinguishing of them in many countries abroad has brought home to us their importance for democratic government. We have seen from recent history that dictators rarely launch a direct attack upon the formal governmental institutions until they have first prepared the way for such an attack by extinguishing the civil liberties of the people.

In addition to civil liberties, democracy requires a popularly elected legislative assembly to draft legislation in response to the people's will. To insure that such an assembly is representative of the people, there must be some fair means of apportioning representation, and the elections to such an assembly must be free. There should be no arbitrary impediments to the exercise of the suffrage or to the holding of office. Age, residence, and citizenship requirements are usually the only legal requirements for voting and for holding office. If the elections are to be genuine and free, the voter must be protected as much as possible from coercion and bribery, and the election results protected from fraud and manipulation.

It may be pointed out—indeed, will be pointed out—that arbitrary impediments often are imposed in fact, if not in law, and that coercion, bribery, and fraud are common practices. But our task here is the delineation of the idea of democracy, not the description of actual political practice. If the actual political practice fails to conform to the idea of democracy, then it is not the concept of democracy that is at fault but the practice, and the practice is properly described as undemocratic. Certainly we have to know all that we can know about actual political practices; but if democracy is conceived as being nothing more nor less than what is actually practiced, it is a meaningless term. We do not derive concepts like democracy from political experience, but we use such concepts to understand political experience. Apart from such concepts, political experience could not be interpreted in any meaningful way. This is a digression but, I think, a necessary one. The observation and description of the actual political process is a large, legitimate, and essential part of the study of politics and government, but it is not the whole of that study. The definition of fundamental political concepts and the evaluation of actual practice in terms of these concepts are essential if politics is to be understood in terms of something larger than the practice itself. Certainly we must know, and know in as much detail as possible, how government and politics are in fact carried on; but to stop with this description is to stop short of understanding it. An adequate description itself will necessarily involve evaluation in terms of the purpose which calls government and politics into existence.

But let me return to my immediate task. I have just said that the idea of democracy cannot tolerate the imposition of arbitrary impediments upon popular participation in politics. If such impediments are introduced in the form of discrimination on account of race, color, religious affiliation, or other arbitrary grounds, then they are properly described as undemocratic. Democracy arose in opposition to the idea that participation in government should be limited to those deemed to be specially qualified to govern on account of the possession of wealth or by virtue of noble birth. And in this sense democracy is opposed to the principle of aristocracy. To the extent that aristocracy means government by those who are wealthy or well-born, the principle of aristocracy is clearly incompatible with democracy; but to the extent that aristocracy means government by those best qualified by virtue and capacity to rule, it is not, I think, a principle opposed to democracy.

Some, like Andrew Jackson, have contended that any intelligent citizen can occupy a position of public responsibility and discharge the duties of office as well as anyone else. But neither he nor any modern democrat believes that the best way to select men for public office is by drawing lots. We think of the election process not as a lottery but as a deliberate means of making a selection, of registering a choice. That choice may be, and often is, limited by arbitrary considerations over which the individual voter has little or no control; but the more genuine the opportunity for choice, the more democratic is the election process. Democracy, like every form of government, requires leadership. It differs from other forms of government, in that it does not arbitrarily exclude anyone from a position of leadership. It does not automatically make every man a leader, but it believes in the equality of opportunity for leadership. It insists that leadership must be won in the public forum. It claims to be superior to aristocracies of wealth and birth on the ground that no one who has qualifications for leadership will be excluded from a position of public responsibility by virtue of his poverty or humble birth. It claims to be superior to older aristocratic forms of government, not on the grounds that it does away with the necessity for superior leadership but that it provides opportunities for leadership that were previously denied. It does not deny the aristocratic principle that those best qualified should be in positions of public responsibility, but it removes any arbitrary definitions of quality and puts its trust in the judgment of the electorate. It is a fundamental maxim of democracy, Montesquieu has pointed out, that the people should choose their magistrates; but it does not follow that every citizen should be regarded as qualified for public office. "As most citizens have sufficient ability to choose, though unqualified to be chosen," he wrote, "so the people capable of calling others to account for their administration, are incapable of conducting the administration themselves."[1] The existence of democracy is endangered, Montesquieu believed, when this fact is forgotten: that, although all are qualified to choose, not all are qualified to be chosen.

1. Montesquieu, *Spirit of the Laws*, trans. Thomas Nugent (London, 1823), Book II, chap. 2.

II

As a means of helping to formulate public policy and carrying it out, as a means of making elections meaningful and presenting the electorate with a choice among candidates representing different political points of view, democracy has given rise to the political party. The political party has become an essential democratic institution, and no democracy is conceivable without it. The best definition of a political party is the one given by Burke, when he describes it as "a body of men united, for promoting by their joint endeavors the national interest, upon some particular principle in which they are all agreed."

The political party, both by definition and by its nature, necessarily contemplates the existence of rival political parties, for there will never be unanimous agreement as to the best means of promoting the national interest or the common good. Since the political party exists as the principal means of helping the electorate to choose among conflicting views of the best means of promoting the common good, a one-party system is a contradiction in terms. By the same token, a multiple-party system that is indistinguishable from a multitude of factions or special-interest groups is likewise no true party system. The political party exists not primarily to represent interests but to unite as many interests as possible in terms of a program and principles which are larger than any particular interest. American and British political experience has shown that the two-party system probably works better in terms of uniting particular interests in terms of a larger national interest than does any other; but multiple-party systems have existed and do exist in democratic governments. It is difficult to say at what precise point the multiple-party system loses its character as a genuine party system; but the difficulty of pointing to a precise dividing line should not obscure the inherent tendency of a multiple-party system to disintegrate into anarchy. Professor F. A. Hermens has given considerable attention to this problem and has pointed out that the Continental European practice of proportional representation, which was introduced in an effort to make parliaments more democratically representative, has, in fact, endangered democratic government and was one of the most important political factors in the demise of many democracies.[2]

There is a widely influential school of political science inspired by the work of E. R. Bentley which conceives of politics as the resolution of group interests. For this group, "pressure politics" is the key to the understanding of politics itself, and the older, traditional view of party politics is relegated to the scrap-heap of outmoded theories. This school of thought has uncovered much significant material concerning the nature and effectiveness of lobbying and the activities of pressure groups behind the formal political scene. But the public interest tends to be conceived by this school of thought as having no objective reality, as being simply the mechanistic resolution of forces involved in "pressure politics." The public interest is not an interest transcending particular interests but the resultant of group pressures and the reflection of particular group interests.

No one denies the fact that pressure groups have played an increasingly important role in our political system. The point at issue is not the fact of "pressure politics" but its meaning. It may be interpreted to mean that politics never was, is not now, and never can be anything other than "pressure politics"; or it may be interpreted as the expression of a politics that has degenerated from what politics by its nature ought to be. If pressure politics is the only kind of politics there ever was or ever can be, then democracy as we have traditionally conceived of it is an impossibility. The function of our government as Madison, for example, conceived it in the tenth number of the *Federalist* is an impossibility. Does government exist to control the effects of factionalism, as he and others thought, or is it simply the reflection of what factions want and are able to get? Perhaps this

2. *Democracy or Anarchy?* (Notre Dame, Ind., 1941).

growing factionalism, which today is called "pressure politics," means that our democratic government is slowly disintegrating into anarchy. To call "pressure politics" democracy, because it is what is actually practiced, will not prevent our democratic government from being destroyed if democracy is, in fact, something else. By equating pressure politics with the democratic process, we obscure the danger to democratic government and lull ourselves into a false complacency. Fortunately for the continued existence of our democratic institutions, the political party is still a reality and, within limits, is still able to unite for political purposes conflicting individual and group interests.

Members of the "pressure-group" school of politics are inclined to reject Burke's definition of the political party as being too "idealistic," for the reason that it emphasizes principles rather than interests. But, in reality, if men are to unite, it must be in terms of principles rather than in terms of interests. As Woodrow Wilson once prophetically said in the debate over the establishment of the League of Nations, "Interests never unite men; interests can only divide." Only purpose can unite men, a purpose that transcends interest. It is only when we are willing to modify or sacrifice our particular interests in terms of a larger purpose that we are able to unite with other men in a common endeavor. It is some conception of the "good life" that animates us to sacrifice our interests when we do, and it is only in terms of some agreement upon the principles of what "the good life" consists that we are enabled to unite with other men.

Political experience would show, I think, that the political party system in America has worked reasonably well in integrating conflicting sectional, economic, and other group interests in terms at least of a national program. It does not always succeed and has failed conspicuously in the formation of tariff legislation, for example, and in yielding to pressure from the farm bloc, but it has often succeeded in formulating and carrying out a program that was something more than the resultant of group pressures.

56 THE MORAL FOUNDATION OF DEMOCRACY

The program is not always exactly the one which is announced in official party platforms at election time, but neither is it so different from those platforms that it bears no resemblance to them. The greater the correspondence between party pronouncements and party action, the more democratic the system is likely to be. To the extent that the party system does, in fact, fail to integrate conflicting interests, as it has in some conspicuous instances, this represents a failure both of the party system and of democratic government.

In instances of this kind, where practice often falls short of theory, the question is: Shall we accept the practice as normative and definitive, or shall we evaluate the practice in terms of principles and make whatever efforts we can to bring our practice more in line with our theory? To accept the practice as normative and definitive seems to me to accept the impossibility of democracy without trying. And it raises the question of whether the legitimate function of the political scientist stops with the description of the practice or whether he has an obligation as a political scientist to evaluate that practice and suggest means by which it might be improved. The political scientist is a man and a citizen, and I do not see how he can accept the first alternative without repudiating his humanity and his responsibility as a citizen. He may seek to keep his obligations as a political scientist, as a man, and as a citizen in watertight compartments; but it would be difficult, to say the least, even for him to tell us when he ceases to be a political scientist and becomes a man or a citizen, or when he thinks in terms of one set of principles appropriate to his science, in terms of another appropriate to his humanity, and in terms of yet another when he thinks as a citizen. But this again is a digression.

III

I have mentioned some of the more important political institutions that are characteristic of democratic government. There are others. Democracy requires a popularly elected legislative assembly to translate policy into legislation for the common good. Because of the size and complexity of modern society, pure democracy is an impossibility except, perhaps, as it survives in local government in the form of the town meeting. Modern democratic government is representative government. And representation is usually apportioned according to population along geographical lines. There are some who advocate forms of functional or occupational representation as being more democratic, but the argument against it is similar to that which has been advanced against proportional representation. Both proportional and functional representation encourage divisiveness and encourage the inherent democratic tendency toward anarchy. Geographical representation has the advantage of forcing particular interests to unite in terms of a larger purpose, since the emphasis is placed upon the individual as a citizen rather than upon the individual as the member of a particular interest group. Geographical representation is no assurance that individuals will not think more in terms of their economic or vocational interests than in larger national terms, but at least it encourages the individual to take a broader view. By conferring representation upon individuals as citizens rather than as members of a particular economic group, it encourages individuals to think and to act as citizens with larger interests. Whether they do or not is another question.

The function of the legislative assembly is not only fairly to represent the people but to deliberate upon public policy and arrive at those decisions dictated by political prudence which will best promote the common good. The legislative assembly has both representative and deliberative functions. There has been a tendency in recent years for the deliberative function of legislative assemblies to be subordinated both in theory and in practice to the representative function. It has been pointed out that very little actual deliberation, for example, takes place on the floor of our Congress and that legislative decisions tend more and more to reflect external pressures. Legislation, it is said, is more often a product of "logrolling," "back-scratching," and other similar practices than it is a product of rational reflection and deliberation. The question again is, How is this development to be interpreted? Is it to be taken as a normative description of what the legislative process really is or as a perversion of that process? If democracy implies government by persuasion and deliberation, then to the extent that a government subordinates deliberation to external pressures, it is not genuinely democratic. If legislation is to have the true character of law, it must be not simply the expression of the will of the legislators but a reflection of rational deliberation. If democratic parliaments throughout the world have increasingly become "will-organizations" rather than "thought-organizations," as some students of government believe, then I would interpret this development as an indication that democracy as a form of government based upon persuasion and deliberation is everywhere in decline. But, fortunately, I think this view, although it contains a great deal of truth, is exaggerated. If debate on the floor of our Congress is often bombastic and futile, it is also true that a great deal of genuine thought and deliberation, real sifting of evidence, and an earnest desire to frame the best policy often take place in committees and outside the formal legislative framework. In our zeal to uncover what might be called the "seamy" side of politics, it should not be forgotten that a great deal of rational deliberation also goes into the framing of legislation, which, although less dramatic, is no less real.

A question that frequently arises in connection with legislative assemblies is the extent to which the individual representative should reflect the views of his constituents and mirror their interests. Does democratic government demand that the representative consider himself a deputy of his constituents acting in accordance with mandates issued by them, or is he free to exercise independence of judgment? The best answer to that question has probably been given by Burke. Speaking to the electors of Bristol in 1774 he said:

My worthy colleague says, his will ought to be subservient to yours. If that be all, the thing is innocent. If government were a matter of will upon any side, yours, without question, ought to be superior. But government and legislation are matters of reason and judgment, and not of inclination; and what sort of reason is that, in which the determination precedes the discussion; in which one set of men deliberate, and another decide. . . . To deliver an opinion is the right of all men; that of constituents is a weighty and respectable opinion, which a representative ought always to rejoice to hear; and which he ought always most seriously to consider. But *authoritative* instructions; *mandates* issued, which the member is bound blindly and implicitly to obey, to vote, and to argue for, though contrary to the clearest conviction of his judgment and conscience,—these are things utterly unknown to the laws of this land, and arise from a fundamental mistake of the whole order and tenor of our constitution.

Parliament is not a *congress* of ambassadors from different and hostile interests; which interests each must maintain, as an agent and advocate, against other agents and advocates; but parliament is a *deliberative* assembly of *one* nation, with *one* interest, that of the whole; where, not local purposes, not local prejudices, ought to guide, but the general good, resulting from the general reason of the whole.[3]

The lobbies, special-interest groups, and blocs that play such a prominent role in the modern legislative process; the use of public opinion polls as oracles of wisdom and as weapons with which to coerce legislators into action; the sycophancy that characterizes so many modern politicians in their relations with their constituents and their demagogic tactics in securing election, Burke would probably—and rightly—regard as signs of parliamentary decadence. To the extent that deliberation is replaced by will, to the extent that the search for justice is replaced by the search for the best means of gratifying desires, legislation degenerates into arbitrary commands, and obligation gives way to force.

If democracy implies government by persuasion and delibera-

3. *Works* (Bohn ed.; London, 1893), I, 447.

tion, then it is the duty of the legislator to use his best reason and his best judgment in the formulation of public policy, subject to recall by his constituents at periodic intervals if they are dissatisfied with the way in which that judgment has been exercised. Since modern democracy is representative democracy, the responsibility for deliberation falls largely, although not exclusively, upon the representative. The problems of modern government are so complex and so technical, their solution requiring more study than the average citizen can give them and information which is not readily available to him, that the task of actually formulating sound policy must, of necessity, fall upon the shoulders of the elected representative. This is not to say that public debate on the issues confronting the government should not be encouraged, but it is to say that the ultimate decision as to how public policy in the form of legislation should actually be framed is the primary responsibility of the legislator. Devices like the initiative and referendum, although designed to foster more democracy in government, actually defeat that purpose by oversimplifying the task of framing legislation and usurp the legitimate and necessary function of the legislative body. Democracy places its faith in the ability of the average man to select men of sound judgment and good character to perform the functions of the legislator, but it does not demand that we regard every man as a competent legislator.

Since democracy is government by persuasion as well as by deliberation, it implies a reciprocal relationship between those in positions of public responsibility and the electorate. It is the function of those in positions of responsibility not only to deliberate as intelligently as they are able upon the best policy to be pursued in particular situations but to persuade the people that this is actually the best possible policy. Upon their ability to persuade the people and thus gain their consent depends their rightful claim to be in positions of responsibility. Unable to secure popular consent for their policies, they should step down, and the election process is designed to implement that responsibility. Some students of government believe that the parliamentary system of government as it is found, for example, in Great Britain is even more democratic than our own system, since such a system is more directly sensitive and hence responsible to public opinion on political issues. Yet, in practice, it has often been the case in such governments that elections were held not at a time when the policy of the government in power was being challenged by public opinion but at times when public opinion was strong in its support. It is the government in power which decides when elections shall take place, and it is inclined to select a time most propitious to itself.

But whether the form of government be presidential or parliamentary—and each has its peculiar merits—it is ultimately true that each government in power must persuade the electorate of the wisdom of its policy, if it is to remain in power. The more democratic the government, the more it will seek to secure genuine consent for its policies and the more it will refrain from attempts to manufacture consent by the methods of propaganda. The ability to persuade will be measured not by the Sophistic ability to win an argument by any means, fair or foul, not by the ability to sway people emotionally, but rather by the ability to win real conviction by argument. The prevalence of demagoguery is a sign of democratic decadence rather than an essential part of the democratic process. We need to revive, if only for the purposes of evaluation, the traditional distinction between the politician and the statesman. The statesman differs from the ordinary politician, in that he is able to envisage and inspire support for policies that are in the *ultimate*, best interest of the most people, and, however rare he may be, we think of him rightly as the politician par excellence. To the extent that the ordinary politician's vision is limited to that which is immediately expedient, to the extent that he is motivated by narrow, sectional, group, or personal interests, we think of him as a failure; and the more narrow his vision and selfish his aim, the greater the failure. The statesman is concerned with inspiring right action, and the test of his statesmanship is his ability to lead public opinion rather than slavishly to follow it. To lead public opinion does not mean to coerce or to beguile the individuals who make up the public but to persuade them by means of argument. It may be said that this is too idealistic a conception of government and of politics. But it is not, I think, a question of attaining perfection. No democratic government is ever perfectly democratic, it is a question of more or less. And the choice confronting us today is whether we will move in the direction of more democratic government or in the direction of less.

Because democracy is government by persuasion and deliberation, it implies the existence of what in the British political tradition is known as the "loyal opposition." So long as the opposition is attached to the fundamental principles upon which democratic government is based, organized opposition to the prevailing government is not only legitimate but essential to its proper functioning. To depict the opposition as treasonable or as unattached to the national interest or the common good, when it is, in fact, loyal to the fundamental principles of democratic government, is to meet opposition not by argument but by slander. There are tendencies today both in this country and in Great Britain to depict any opposition to the government in power as undemocratic opposition and hence illegitimate, to insist that only the government in power is attached to government by and for the people. To hear some people talk, the Republicans are not really attached to the national interest but are Fascist-minded reactionaries. To hear others talk, the New Deal and Fair Deal Democrats are not really democrats at all but potential Communists in sheep's clothing. Both kinds of insinuations do a disservice to democracy and deny the concept and practice of loyal opposition. Undoubtedly, there are reactionaries among conservatives and radicals among liberals, both of whom would lead us, if in power, to dangerous extremes; but in our zeal to ferret out the reactionaries and the radicals we should not lose sight in our partisanship of the necessity for and desirability of legitimate opposition within democratic government of genuine conservative and liberal points of view. *The more we resort to slander and the less we rely upon argument, the weaker our democracy and the more uncertain its future.*

IV

Democratic government is also constitutional government. We could have and have had constitutional governments which were not democratic, but we cannot have a genuine democratic government which is not a constitutional one. There are differences of opinion among students of government as to what constitutional government means. It is clear that the existence of constitutional government does not depend upon a written constitution. The U.S.S.R. has a written constitution but is not a constitutional government. Great Britain, on the other hand, has no single document called the "constitution" but is a constitutional government. The opposite of constitutional government is tyranny, and one of the essential characteristics of constitutional government is the existence of effective limitations upon the powers and functions of government. Under the constitutional form of government there are some things which the government is absolutely forbidden to do. Professor Friedrich has defined a constitution as a system of effective, regularized restraints upon governmental action. This is satisfactory as far as it goes, but it leaves unanswered the question "restrained in terms of what?" There is a sense in which even tyrants feel restrained, although it may be argued that those restraints are not regularized and often are not effective. Traditionally, constitutionalism has been defined in terms of restraints imposed by law, and the Constitution has been described as the fundamental law of the land. This seems to me to be both historically and philosophically a sounder conception of constitutionalism. Professor C. H. McIlwain declares that the essence of constitutional government is the recognition of the existence of "a law that puts bounds to arbitrary will."[4] The opposite of constitutional government is not autocracy, which is "unmixed government," but rather despotism, that is, "lawless government." Although, in practice, autocracy and despotism tend to merge, they are not identical. "As moderns," Professor McIlwain writes, ". . . we tend to fix our attention on the legitimacy of an act of government, where the ancients looked merely to its desirability or expediency." And he adds that "such an idea of legitimacy could only arise after men had come to think of a universal law which had more coercive power than mere universal reason, but, like reason, was coterminous with mankind; and, what is more, coeval with man himself. And granted that there was such a pre-existent law, it became inevitable that governments and their acts should be judged by their conformity to it rather than to reason alone."[5] Constitutional government is a practical manifestation and reflection of the idea of natural law. Constitutional government is a kind of self-restraint which the people in a democracy impose upon themselves; and, whether we have institutions of judicial review or not, its continued existence depends less upon the institutional checks provided than upon the commonly shared knowledge that there are restraints and upon willingness of individuals voluntarily to submit to those restraints. Constitutional government, conceived as government restrained by the dictates of a law more fundamental than that enacted by the legislature, is an essential characteristic of democratic government.

V

I have mentioned what seem to me to be some of the essential institutional characteristics of democratic government. There are

4. "The Fundamental Law behind the Constitution of the United States," in Conyers Read (ed.), *The Constitution Reconsidered* (New York, 1938), p. 3. Quoted with permission of the Columbia University Press.

5. *Ibid.*, p. 5.

others, but these are certainly among the more important. It should be remembered that democratic government is composed of a number of institutions, no one of which can be isolated from the others as the essential institution of democracy and all of which are necesary to its proper functioning. It is also important to realize that the mere existence of these institutions is no guaranty of their continued existence. It is the way in which they are conceived and the way in which they are used that will ultimately determine their efficacy as instruments of freedom. They are a means to freedom, we believe an indispensable means, but they are not identical with freedom itself.

There is no democratic institution which is not subject to perversion, and the spirit in which we employ these institutions, therefore, is as important as are the institutions themselves. The collapse of democratic government in many European countries in recent years should be warning enough that the democratic process itself carries with it no assurance of its continued existence. Free elections may be utilized by demagogues as well as by statesmen. They may be the means by which those who are best qualified by virtue and capacity to hold positions of public responsibility are selected, or they may be the means by which a political movement, such as the Fascist or the Communist, seizes the reins of government and puts an end to free elections. Free elections, as we saw in Germany before Hitler's rise to power, were no guaranty against the rise of tyranny. Nor were popularly elected legislative assemblies. Hitler's dictatorial powers were originally conferred upon him by a vote of the German Reichstag and, even with the Communists expelled and the Socialists voting against the Enabling Act, by a large enough majority of the total membership at least technically to meet the constitutional provision requiring a two-thirds vote for the amendment of the Weimar Constitution.

There are some who will say that it cannot happen here, because America is protected from that fate by a tradition which excludes it as a possibility. A tradition, however, is no more effective than the convictions of those living today who believe in it and understand it. A tradition may inspire us to thought and action, but it cannot take the place of thought and action. A tradition may sustain us in our convictions, but it cannot take the place of convictions.

If democracy survives as a form of government, it will be not simply because it has become strong enough in a military and economic sense to resist the threat of aggression and annihilation but because it is essential to the political implementation of a philosophy of life which demands it. We are too much inclined to think that the preservation of freedom is primarily a matter of increasing military production and planning appropriate military strategy. There are indications that we are placing more reliance upon industrial, technological, and military superiority than such superiority in itself can ever justify. Powerful we must be if we are successfully to meet the challenge with which communism confronts us throughout the world; but if we are successfully to enlist the active support of our own people and of other peoples throughout the world, we shall need, in addition to the weapons of war, the resolution to endure suffering for the sake of something we prize more highly than physical existence alone. If we value our physical existence more than we value our freedom, we cannot successfully defeat an aggressor who values his philosophical and political convictions above his life.

The preservation and defense of freedom cannot be simply equated with the military defense of our national integrity or with the preservation of the status quo, whether domestic or international. The danger is that we may forget that our industrial, military, and technological effort, however essential to the preservation of freedom, is not identical with it. We may mistake the means for the end; and unless we are motivated by a desire for a freedom which is spiritually and intellectually articulate, we may lose our freedom in the very process of building up the "garrison state" to defend it. If we are to preserve our freedom at home and extend it throughout the world, it must be in terms of a conception of freedom which is universal, dynamic, and creative. The world in which we live is in revolutionary ferment; and a Maginot-line mentality which seeks safety in the preservation of the status quo cannot help being outflanked and outmaneuvered by those who are motivated by a missionary zeal. Self-defense is not enough. Freedom must lead to creative activity or perish. If freedom is interpreted to mean "leave me in peace," if it cannot see beyond the defense of existing political boundaries and the preservation of the status quo, if it cannot enlist and support the energies of those peoples throughout the world who are determined upon revolutionary change, it cannot long survive. Nikolai Berdyaev put the matter simply when he wrote: "Liberty will be saved by its union with Truth—it cannot be saved by indifference to Truth. Freedom means not only freedom of choice, but choice itself. . . ."[6]

Our democratic institutions require a philosophy of life to sustain them. They are the means to freedom, but they are not identical with it. The important thing is how we conceive of this freedom and what we propose to do with it. Even more formidable than the threat of Russian aggression is our lack of a philosophy in terms of which we can justify our democracy and our preference for it. For without a clear understanding of why these institutions exist, we shall have neither the means of defending them intellectually nor the resolution to defend them by force when the occasion demands it. The means for victory over tyranny are abundant; only the ends are obscure.

6. *The Fate of Man in the Modern World* (London, 1935), p. 46.

IV. Democracy and Liberalism

Historically considered, the relationship between liberalism and democracy is an intimate one; for modern democratic government and liberalism developed concomitantly. Both have their roots in the seventeenth century; and, ever since the seventeenth century, democracy as a form of government has been sustained by liberalism as a political and social philosophy. So intimate has this connection been that democracy and liberalism are often spoken of as equivalent terms. But today everywhere throughout the world liberalism is in decline or on the defensive. And one question, therefore, presents itself with more and more insistence, namely: Can democracy as a form of government survive the demise of liberalism as the dominant political and social philosophy? Before attempting an answer to that question, however, I should like first to review briefly the meaning of liberalism and the reason for its decline.

I

Liberalism was the product of the climate of opinion that emerged at the time of the Renaissance and the Reformation. The period of the Renaissance and the Reformation accelerated an intellectual movement that had its roots in the later Middle Ages. Interest in classical literature and civilization was stimulated as men sought to find in antiquity patterns of thought and a way of life applicable to the new situation that was characterized by the crumbling of the universal church, the rise of the nation-state, and the disintegration of the feudal economy.

In the Middle Ages there was no clear-cut separation of private and public spheres of activity. There was no state in the modern sense of that word and hence no distinction between the "state" and "society." Feudalism, as a system of reciprocal rights and duties, was based upon personal, legal relationships organized hierarchically. The distinction between political authority and personal rights was blurred. But with the disintegration of the feudal order, prerogatives of rulership, which had earlier been thought of as the private property of the ruler, were gradually transferred to the sphere of public administration. By virtue of the peculiar circumstances of the times, political authority necessitated the introduction of general systems of taxation, the creation of bureaucracies, and the employment of standing armies. Thus, gradually, the prerogatives of rulership became impersonalized. And when there was attached to these new phenomena the concept of *raison d'état*, the idea of the modern state emerged.

As a consequence of this impersonalization of the political order, the individual acquired a sphere of autonomy such as he had never known in medieval society. This sphere, which now corresponded to "society," was set apart from the impersonal, public, political order, which was the "state." The medieval problem of the relationship between ecclesiastical and secular authority was never solved but was replaced in immediate importance by the problem of the relationship between state and society, between the spheres of political authority and individual autonomy. Liberalism emerged as a specific answer to this problem.

It was the Renaissance that produced the concept of the autonomous individual, or the "masterless man." While the new conception of individuality drew heavily upon ancient Greece, and especially Stoicism, for its inspiration, it was not simply a reiteration of Greek ideas about man but, indeed, a new conception. Professor Reinhold Niebuhr has emphasized the novelty of this idea:

If Protestantism represents the final heightening of the idea of in-dividuality within terms of the Christian religion, the Renaissance is the real cradle of that very unchristian concept and reality: the au-tonomous individual. . . . Ostensibly Renaissance thought is a re-vival of classicism, the authority of which is either set against the authority of Christianity or used to modify the latter. Yet classic thought has no such passion for the individual as the Renaissance betrays. The fact is that the Renaissance uses an idea which could have grown only upon the soil of Christianity. It transplants this idea to the soil of classic rationalism to produce a new concept of individual autonomy, which is known in neither classicism nor Christianity.[1]

And Professor G. H. Sabine says:

. . . Convinced that it must start from what was self-evident, mod-ern philosophy could find nothing apparently so solid and indubitable as individual human nature. The individual human being, with his interests, his enterprise, his desire for happiness and advancement, above all with his reason, which seemed the condition for a successful use of all his other faculties, appeared to be the foundation on which a stable society must be built. Traditional differences of status already began to seem precarious. Not man as a priest or a soldier, as the member of a guild or an estate, but man as a bare human being, a "masterless man," appeared to be the solid fact.[2]

Based upon a conception of individuality that emphasized the autonomy of individual will, the autonomy of human reason, and the essential goodness and perfectibility of human nature, liberal-ism was the political expression of this individualistic Weltan-schauung. Individual freedom was its major premise and its goal. The freedom it sought was freedom from all authority that was capable of acting capriciously or arbitrarily.

The problem of securing individual freedom was not only a theoretical problem but a practical one. For the individual of the

1. *The Nature and Destiny of Man* (2 vols.; New York, 1941), I, 61. Quoted with permission of Charles Scribner's Sons.

2. *History of Political Theory* (2d ed.; New York, 1950), p. 432. Quoted with the permission of Henry Holt and Company.

seventeenth century was, in fact, hedged in and restrained politically, socially, and economically by arbitrary, personal authority. These restraints not only impeded the expansion and development of free, private economic enterprise but were also incompatible in principle with the basic liberal postulate of the essential moral worth and equality of human personality. It was the rising commercial class that felt these restraints most keenly, and liberalism was its challenge to political absolutism. At first, it is true, the commercial class supported absolute monarchy in the interest of national unity; but, as that class became stronger and more self-assertive, it chafed under the arbitrary restraints imposed by the absolute monarchy and led the rebellion against it.

In order to realize its conception of individual freedom, the commercial class needed such freedoms as freedom of expression, freedom of assembly, freedom from arbitrary arrest and imprisonment. It needed a voice in the shaping of governmental policy. But if civil liberties and representative government were tactically desirable, they were also a logical outgrowth of the liberal philosophy. Liberalism was at one and the same time a theoretical intellectual attitude and a practical expression of rebellion against concrete restraints and specific injustices. In their own minds the early liberals did not separate, as some modern interpreters of their philosophy are inclined to do, their social and economic motives and aspirations from their intellectual convictions. Liberalism was not simply, as it is sometimes said to be, the embodiment of a demand for economic freedom but the embodiment of a demand for freedom in every sphere of life—intellectual, social, economic, political, and religious—and it is doubtful whether the early liberal prized one more highly than the other or even considered that he might enjoy one kind of freedom without the others. If the commercial class rebelled with vigor against arbitrary economic restraints, it protested with equal fervor and conviction against arbitrary political power, star-chamber proceedings, *lettres de cachet*, restrictions upon freedom of expression and upon religious worship. If it opposed an aristocracy of birth, it was not simply as parvenus but as a matter of principle.

The central problem with which liberalism was concerned was the relation between the individual and authority. How could the notion of individual equality and autonomy be reconciled with the necessity for political authority? How could individuals conceived as having absolute and equal rights submit to political authority without denying the absoluteness or equality of their claims? If the individual, because of the absolute value of human personality, cannot submit to any personal authority capable of acting capriciously and arbitrarily, to what authority can he submit? And the liberal answered: He can submit only to the authority of law; it alone can command and restrain him. Accordingly, liberalism advocates freedom from every form of social control except law. As it was to be put succinctly by Voltaire in the eighteenth century: "Freedom consists in being independent from everything but law."

Latent within liberalism are two self-sufficient and logically independent notions of law. Merged by the force of historical circumstance into one conception, their mutual inconsistency and independence were not at first recognized. First of all, there is the notion that law is the product of individual wills and the expression of subjective interests. Second, there is the notion retained from the Middle Ages that law is the embodiment of eternal truths and values discoverable by reason. In the first case it is the sheer compulsion behind the law, in the last analysis, that makes the individual submit to it; in the second case, it is the rational recognition of the rightness of the content of the law that imposes obligation. The source of law is thought of, in the first instance, as individual wills; in the second, as reason. The validity of law rests, in the former conception, upon the fact that the competent authority, possessed of superior coercive power, has prescribed it. In the latter conception the validity of law rests upon its content, upon its inherent rightness or justice. The bases of validity are, on the one hand, formal and, on the other, substantive. So long as liberalism retains both notions, it retains its integral character; but, with the formalization of liberal concepts, with the gradual abandonment of the substantive conception of law, when the formal conception of law alone is retained, liberalism becomes degenerate, preparing the way for its own destruction. For a purely formal limitation is no limitation at all.

Liberalism conceived of society as being composed of atom-like, autonomous individuals with wills and interests peculiar to themselves. But to this anarchic conception of society it counterposed the belief in the existence of a transcendental order of truth which is accessible to man's natural reason and capable of evoking a moral response. But how is it certain that the individual will not will that which is subjectively desired rather than that which is objectively demanded? There is no certainty. For, ultimately, liberalism acknowledges no limitation upon individual will except that which is imposed by individual conscience. Order, then, is potentially embodied in the existence of objective truth discoverable by natural reason; but, in the final analysis, it is conscience alone that bids the individual to reason objectively, to discover the true content of law, to translate this potential order into actuality. The whole obligation for realizing order rests upon the individual, and, more specifically, upon individual conscience. Conscience, therefore, is the keystone of the liberal structure. Only conscience bids the individual to follow the dictates of reason rather than those of interest, and upon the conscientiousness of individuals alone rests the choice between order and anarchy. The true law to which individuals owe obedience, the law under which freedom is assured, is that law whose content is found in individual conscience. Duty alone connects the natural liberty of the individual with the objective order. The gap between subjective reality and objective ideality is bridged in liberalism by the sense of obligation. The whole obligation for realizing order rests upon individual thought and will, and individual will is the dynamic factor which is capable of creating either order or anarchy.

Liberalism, then, was based upon an uneasy compromise between two conflicting principles: the idea of the autonomy of individual will and reason and the idea of a higher law. The appeal to conscience that was supposed to reconcile these two conflicting principles proved in time to be without weight or sanction. At best, it was an appeal to a Christian ethic that could not long survive the repudiation of the Christian religion. For the conscience that was to reconcile the two conflicting principles was essentially the Christian conscience, and that conscience could not survive the separation of reason from faith and the repudiation of the authority of the church. Cut loose from its moorings in faith, reason drifted with the tides of opinion, no longer able to distinguish the true from the false, the good from the bad, the just from the unjust. What appeared "self-evidently" true to the seventeenth-century mind that was still close to the medieval, Christian tradition was destined to appear increasingly less self-evident as the mind of man progressively "freed" itself from the Christian revelation and the authority of the church.

II

Of the many factors which have contributed to the decline of liberalism, probably the most important intellectual factor was the rise of positivism and its infiltration into practically all realms of thought. During the nineteenth century the natural sciences achieved an unprecedented prestige. And the practical application of scientific discoveries seemed to many to herald the dawn of millennium. Where men had formerly looked to God for the salvation of their souls, they now looked to science and technology for the gratification of their desires. The method had been found: paradise on earth waited only upon the proper execution of a plan to be discovered in the truths and with the methods of the natural sciences.

Social scientists, seeking to emulate the natural sciences, were captivated by the idea of achieving for the study of social phenomena the same calculable certainty that characterized the physical sciences. Turning to the study of human and social phenomena with concepts borrowed, often indiscriminately, from the physical sciences, the social scientists believed that they were upon the threshold of discovering—if, indeed, they had not already discovered—the "laws" of social progress. Progress was conceived as automatic, inevitable, and irreversible.

Now positivism is an attitude growing out of the natural sciences but is not, indeed, synonymous with the scientific method. It is a perspective, moreover, which is more common to social scientists than it is to natural scientists. Guido de Ruggiero defines positivism as "a philosophical tendency oriented around natural science and striving for a unified view of the world of phenomena, both physical and human, through the application of the methods and the extension of the results whereby the natural sciences have attained their unrivaled position in the modern world." It represents the complete victory of empiricism and "calls 'positive' the facts and things of immediate perception as well as the relations and uniformities which thought may discover in them without transcending experience." It regards as metaphysical "every inquiry which claims to go beyond the sphere of the empirical and seeks either hidden essences behind phenomenal appearances, or ultimate efficient and final causes behind things, as well as any attempt to attribute reality to species, ideas, concepts or the mind's logical 'intentions' in general."[3] It is an attempt to limit the validity of reason in the search for truth to the methods of the natural sciences and to discard all metaphysical speculation and ethical evaluation as being scientifically irrelevant.

3. "Positivism," in the *Encyclopedia of the Social Sciences* (New York, 1934), XII, 260.

Truth is regarded by the positivist simply as that which can be described inductively from the empirical observation of successive events. The positivist's belief in causation and in a progress inevitably decreed by nature or by history illustrates, however, that metaphysical speculation, far from being abandoned, is indulged in unconsciously and uncritically. Instead of eliminating metaphysical speculation and ethical evaluation, the positivist simply removes them from the scrutiny of reason by obscuring even from himself the speculation and evaluation that must, of necessity, enter into his descriptive endeavors. Surreptitious speculation and evaluation are then often proclaimed as the latest discovery of "science." Thus science is used, or rather misused, to lend prestige to ideas whose origin is not in nature or in science but in the uncritical mind of the person promulgating them.

Now when liberal ideas were focused from the perspective of positivism, they underwent a significant change in content, if not in form. The liberal vocabulary of the nineteenth century remained substantially the same as the liberal vocabulary of the seventeenth; but what the nineteenth-century liberal understood by the basic liberal concepts was something quite different from what his seventeenth-century predecessor had understood by them.

The positivist tends to regard all value judgments as expressions simply of subjective individual preference. He denies that value judgments refer to any objective reality, because he cannot scientifically demonstrate the existence of anything like a moral order. He concludes, since he clings to the method of natural science as the only valid method of discovering truth, that there is no moral law or moral order. Dominated by empiricism, he is inclined to avoid all qualitative judgments as subjective and to rely, instead, upon quantitative measurement and methods of thought to which alone he attaches objectivity. His inability to measure values quantitatively lends, he believes, further validity to his argument for rejecting them as facts.

Since the positivist cannot empirically demonstrate the existence of a "soul," he tends to concentrate upon man as being primarily a physical organism. And those spiritual aspects of man which do not lend themselves to scientific description and observation are pushed further and further into the background until they tend to disappear entirely from view. With this perspective the positivist cannot empirically demonstrate the moral worth or spiritual equality of individuals, and for the idea of substantive equality he is forced to substitute a purely formal equality. The premise of the absolute moral worth of the individual, which lay at the foundation of liberalism as originally conceived, is thus denied. If the positivist clings to such a conception, it must be as a kind of irrational bias or subjective preference.

And for the transcendent order potentially embodied in reason and conscience, the positivist liberal substituted the conception of an immanent order of nature. The transcendent order of classical liberalism required individual effort (both thought and action) for its realization; the immanent order substituted for it is conceived as being already in existence and hence requiring neither thought nor effort for its actualization. Individuals, it was believed, could discover the laws of this immanent order by scientific methods, but these laws would remain in operation whether discovered or not. Men might accelerate the natural process by discovering the laws of its operation; but the attainment of social order did not ultimately depend upon either the thoughts or the actions of individuals. When the methods of natural science were substituted in the nineteenth century for the seventeenth-century conception of "right reason," social laws exactly analogous to the physical laws of nature were substituted for the natural law of reason, and men looked for order not in reason but in some natural or historical process. No matter what men might think, believe, or do, the immanent laws of "nature" or of "history" would control their destiny. It was a comfortable belief, particularly when it was linked with the never explained metaphysical assumption that the "laws" of "nature" or of "history" inevitably and automatically impel men along the road to progress. It led to a smug complacency that has only recently been shattered. By relieving the individual of all responsibility for social progress, freedom tended, for all practical purposes, to degenerate into license.

When the classical liberal theory of law was subjected to the positivist's scrutiny, only the subjective part of that theory survived. As Roscoe Pound has observed: "The old natural law called for search for an eternal body of principles to which the positive law must be made to conform. This new natural law called for search for a body of rules governing legal development, to which law will conform, do what we may. . . . The most man may do is to observe and, thus, it may be, to learn to predict. For the rest nature will take her inexorable course and we may but impotently wring our hands."[4] And Professor E. S. Corwin has observed that when the scientific conception of "natural law" in the sense of "the observed order of phenomena" was substituted for the earlier rationalistic conception, this aided "the triumph of the idea of human and governmental law as an expression solely of will backed by force."[5] Justice, being a metaphysical concept, was discarded by the positivist as being empirically worthless. And since reason was denied the capacity of discovering the principles of justice, its function was confined to an analysis of the existing law, in the belief that positive law is the only true law. The criteria of law became the manner of enactment and the force behind it. Any command that issued from a legislature or other organ of government empowered to issue commands in accordance with a prescribed procedure with sufficient force behind it to compel obedience was law and the only true law. Freedom under the law was retained by the positivist liberal as

4. *The Spirit of the Common Law* (Boston, 1921), p. 163.

5. "The 'Higher Law' Background of American Constitutional Law," *Harvard Law Review*, XLII (1928), 382, note.

an article of his liberal faith, but it came to mean something quite different from what it had originally meant. Originally it had meant that a man could not be compelled to do anything contrary to reason or conscience, that the test of a law was its justness. Under the influence of positivism, the concept came to mean that a man could not be compelled to do anything except by a law enacted in accordance with a prescribed procedure (any prescribed procedure) with sufficient force behind it to compel obedience. Now there is a great difference between freedom from *unjust* compulsion and freedom from *illegal* compulsion, especially when the notion of legality is divorced from justice and when the test of legality is ultimately conceived as the force behind the law. Freedom from illegal compulsion means, then, for all practical purposes, no more than freedom to do whatever the state has not yet forbidden. This is a conception of freedom more congenial to tyranny than to the preservation of the inalienable rights of man.

But the conception of the inalienable rights of man no more survived the scrutiny of positivism than did the concept of justice. Viewed from the perspective of positivism, the rights of man are conceived no longer as natural rights, belonging to an individual by virtue of his humanity, but simply as legal rights, belonging to him by virtue of his relationship to the state. Properly speaking, according to the positivistic point of view, man has no rights at all; what the liberals have traditionally called "rights" are actually only concessions granted by the state. Whatever rights an individual has are those guaranteed by positive law; and, since the rights are the product of the law, they are not, properly speaking, rights at all but concessions to claims which the individual makes and the state recognizes. As concessions, they may be withdrawn or limited as the state thinks fit.[6]

6. This thesis is supported with greater evidence than could be supplied here in my *Decline of Liberalism as an Ideology* (Berkeley, 1943) and is further elucidated in my *Main Currents in Modern Political Thought* (New York, 1950).

It was the liberal, positivist jurists long before Hitler who taught (explicitly or implicitly) that might makes right, that rights are not attributes which individuals possess by virtue of their humanity but simply claims which the state may or may not choose to recognize. And such liberals, unwittingly it may be, prepared the way for Lidice and Dachau. And the same positivistically inspired intellectual forces are at work in our own country.

III

If it be conceded for the purpose of this discussion that the rise of positivism has led to the degeneration of liberalism, what is to happen to the democracy that has long been sustained by it? If our thinking continues to be dominated by positivism, I believe, for the reasons indicated, that it can lead only to the destruction of democracy and the rise of tyranny. But suppose we repudiate the perspective of positivism. Should we return to the principles of classical liberalism? Certainly there are insights in classical liberalism which should be recovered, but there are also errors. The intellectual task of our generation is to find and formulate a political and social philosophy that can retain the truth in liberalism and transcend its errors.

Many of the ideas embodied in liberalism are not peculiar to liberalism but have a long heritage in the history of Western civilization, and these ideas must be recovered in any adequate political philosophy. The beliefs, for example, in the absolute moral worth of the individual, in the spiritual equality of individuals, and in the essential rationality of man were a heritage from the Middle Ages and have their roots deep in Christian and Greek thought. We can repudiate these ideas only by repudiating our humanity. It is the belief in the absolute moral worth of the individual that prevents the individual from being submerged, if not obliterated, in a conception of the race, the class, the nation, or some other collectivity that regards the individual as a means rather than as an end in himself. It is in terms of the conception of the spiritual equality of individuals that we can understand the words in the Declaration of Independence that "all men are created equal" and strive toward the attainment of equality of opportunity for all men. Individuals are not equal in any empirical sense; and, so long as our thinking is restricted to that which is empirically demonstrable, the phrase "all men are created equal" must appear as nonsense. The phrase derived originally from the belief that all men are created equal in the sight of God, that the souls of men are equally precious to God, and that all individuals should be treated with the respect due to a creature made in the image and likeness of God. It is this belief in the sacredness of human life which leads us to sustain the lives of the most hopelessly crippled in mind and body, which prevents us from performing those experiments on human beings, even in the interest of science, which the Nazis, for example, performed with callous indifference. Because individuals are equal in a spiritual sense, they are entitled to the same opportunities for the realization of their potentialities as human beings, and no arbitrary barriers to that equality of opportunity, though they exist, can be justified. God's image in man is reflected in the capacity of human beings to reason, and the disparagement of that capacity can lead only to the denial of man's uniqueness. And if men persist long enough in proclaiming that they are not essentially different from animals, they cannot very well complain when they are treated like animals. Professor Étienne Gilson has pointed out:

Man is best described as a rational animal; deprive man of reason, and what is left is not man, but animal. This looks like a very commonplace statement, yet Western culture is dying wherever it has been forgotten; for the rational nature of man is the only conceivable foundation for a rational system of ethics. Morality is essentially normality; for a rational being to act and to behave either without reason or contrary to its dictates is to act and behave, not exactly as a beast, but as a beastly man, which is worse. For it is proper that a beast should act as a beast, that is, according to its own nature;

but it is totally unfitting for a man to act as a beast, because that means the complete oblivion of his own nature, and hence his final destruction.[7]

Man is not an animal upon whom reason has been grafted, but he is a unique being. "The distinctive mark of humanity as over against materiality and animality," as Professor Helmut Kuhn has pointed out, is not "a power or faculty residing in man as merely an additional endowment":

Man, it is true, is capable of achievements beyond the reach of animals. Language and rational thought are given him alone. But if we understand the ancient definition of man as *animal rationale* in that sense (not the sense intended by its originators), it defines a hybrid rather than man. Nothing more monstrous than an animal, living, feeding, mating, perishing as an animal but endowed with intelligence. Only a dehumanized man may approach this condition. Rather than being engrafted upon animality, the distinctively human element must inform and transfigure animality. Man is human not only by virtue of his ratiocinative power. He calls his matings marriage, his be-getters parents, his feeding taking meals, and, conscious of life, he foresees the oncoming death. For better or for worse, he is an altogether unique being, projecting as it were, into a dimension foreign to animality. All this is not said in confutation of the idea that ra-

7. *The Unity of Philosophical Experience* (New York, 1937), p. 274. Quoted with permission of Charles Scribner's Sons. Today science is often appealed to, to do the work of philosophy; but, by reducing philosophy to science, man has abdicated his right not only to judge nature but to rule it. As Gilson says: "Far from making up for the loss of philosophy, the discovery of the scientific substitutes for it leaves man alone with nature such as it is, and obliges him to surrender to natural necessity. Philosophy is the only rational knowledge by which both science and nature can be judged. By reducing philosophy to pure science, man has not only abdicated his right to judge nature and to rule it; but he has also turned himself into a particular aspect of nature, subjected, like all the rest, to the necessary law which regulates its development. A world where accomplished facts are unto themselves their own justification is ripe for the most reckless social adventures. Its dictators can wantonly play havoc with human institutions and human lives, for dictatorships are facts and they also are unto themselves their own justifications" (*ibid.*, p. 277). Quoted with the permission of Charles Scribner's Sons.

tionality is the *differentia specifica* of our race. If only we fight shy of that emasculated idea of reason that infected post-Cartesian philosophy (reason cut loose from passion and debarred from vision), we may find the ancient concept still useful. Or rather it will prove indispensable.[8]

Not only must we recover the belief in man as a unique being whose reason is a reflection of the image of God, but we must also recover our belief in the existence of universally valid principles in terms of which we can guide our individual and social life toward the perfection of that which is distinctively human. The early liberals sought to appropriate the natural law of the Middle Ages without the theological foundations upon which it rested, and this secularization of the law had the effect ultimately of leading to its repudiation.[9] Only by recovering the theological foundations upon which the belief in natural law rests, can we recover the idea of the rule of law which liberalism, because of its thoroughgoing secularism, sought inadequately to perpetuate. The liberal conception of natural rights also needs correction. Although the conception of rights implies correlative duties, liberalism tended to emphasize the inalienable nature of these rights rather than the duties which these rights imply. As a matter of fact, the liberal endeavor to ground these rights in the empirical nature of man, in an effort to divorce them from any dependence upon theological considerations, ignored the fact, which soon became apparent, that such rights are not empirically demon-

8. "Philosophy and Religion: The Humanity of Man," in Loren C. Mac-Kinney *et al., A State University Surveys the Humanities* (Chapel Hill, 1945), pp. 74–75. Quoted with the permission of the University of North Carolina Press.

9. This secularization of the natural law was performed most notably by Hugo Grotius. He did not deny the validity of natural law but sought rather, because of the circumstances of the times in which he lived, to ground that law upon a foundation which would depend neither upon the authority of the church nor upon the authority of Scripture (cf. Sabine, *op. cit.,* pp. 420–33). An excellent, brief discussion of the history of natural law will be found in A. P. D'Entrèves, *Natural Law* (New York, 1951).

strable. In reality, the rights of man derive not from the empirically observable nature of man but from the fact that man is a spiritual being created in the image and likeness of God. Men have rights because they have responsibilities which transcend the demands of the natural world. Because we have a destiny that transcends time and, as a consequence, responsibilities that transcend the demands of the particular time and society in which we live, we must have the freedom proportionate to those responsibilities and the rights that are derived from those obligations. Because rights are correlative to responsibilities, they are never as absolute as the liberal believed but are relative to the way in which such responsibilities are conceived and carried out. Our rights are derived from our obligations.

The atomistic conception of society upon which liberalism erected its theory of the state is also in need of correction. The only basis of civil society which the liberal could conceive was a contract. "No other natural method can be imagined," Grotius declared, whereby individuals may be obligated to one other. Although, as Locke said, reason "teaches all mankind who will but consult it, that . . . no one ought to harm another in his life, health, liberty or possessions," it is only by an act of will that the teachings of reason become practically binding. The individual is conceived as choosing to assume this obligation not to harm another by entering into a contract whereby civil society is established. Although impelled by reason, the decision is a pure act of will. Conceivably, by another act of will he might repudiate this decision. This possibility is not contemplated by Locke because he cannot envisage men acting contrary to the dictates of natural reason. Men might decide to revolt against a tyrannical government, but it is inconceivable to Locke that they would decide to establish a government contrary to the dictates of reason and destructive of natural rights.

The state is regarded not as a natural necessity arising out of men's needs and social nature with a purpose transcending the subjective wills of individuals but as an artificial instrumentality based upon the claims of individuals. The state exists to satisfy men's claims and to reflect their will. This conception did not appear dangerous in any way to the early liberal, for it was inconceivable to him that the will of men could be anything but good or their claims anything other than legitimate. We have witnessed the rise of states in the twentieth century, however, in which the will of men which they reflected was anything but good and the claims they advanced anything but legitimate. And the rise of these states was made possible partly because of the conception of the state which was embodied in classical liberalism. For the conception of the state as an instrumentality of the will of men contains in itself no limitation upon the way in which that will shall be employed. Without the conception of a final end or purpose for which the state exists, the will of men can rapidly degenerate, as it did, in fact, degenerate, into an irresponsible one.

The liberal conception of society ignores the organic nature of community and the fact that individuals require one another *of necessity*. Individuals do not create society but are born into it. Man is by nature a social being who requires the fellowship and services of other men. Man is born into society, and that fact alone imposes obligations upon him; these obligations do not require his formal consent but arise out of a relationship which is natural and essential rather than voluntary. The relation of man to society is like the relation of parent and child; our social obligations rest, like our parental and filial obligations, not upon a matter of choice but upon a matter of fact. Society is not an artificial creation of men, it is not an invention of their reason and an instrumentality of their will, but an organic community with purposes including, but transcending, the purposes of particular individuals.

And every society has its roots in a particular historical tradition. It was one of the weaknesses of liberalism that it tended to ignore these roots and to exalt abstract reason to the neglect of custom and tradition. Thus it tended to foster the dangerous illusion that we can construct a civil society *de novo* and *ex nihilo*. "I cannot conceive," Burke wrote, "how any man can have brought himself to that pitch of presumption, to consider his country as nothing but *carte blanche* upon which he may scribble whatever he pleases. A man . . . may wish his society otherwise constituted than he finds it; but a good patriot and a true politician always considers how he shall make the most of the existing materials of his country. A disposition to preserve and an ability to improve, taken together, would be my standard of a statesman." He pointed out that there is a middle ground between "absolute destruction" and "unreformed existence" and declared that it is the task of the statesman to find that middle ground. To the reason of the individual man Burke wisely opposed the "collected reason" of men of all nations and of all times; and to the abstract Reason exalted by the eighteenth-century *philosophes* he opposed the practical reason of Aristotle. The *philosophes* had an unbounded confidence in man's ability to be persuaded by reason to establish a just social order. Burke emphasized a truth which they neglected—that sentiment plays an even larger role in social life than reason, that "naked reason" unmotivated by the love of what is good and abstracted from the totality of human experience is likely to be turned not only against the good but against reason itself. Political problems are not like problems in geometry, nor can we proceed to construct a social order from a set of a priori assumptions. The materials with which the statesman must work are not counters which can be pushed this way and that in accordance with some preconceived plan but are passionate human beings, capable of co-operation with the good but capable also of rebellion against it. Sentiment, or love, therefore, must always be reckoned with, and it is only by inculcating habits of veneration through institutions that the passions of men can be channelized into socially beneficent action.

A new social philosophy will retain the liberal goal of freedom, but it will temper its passion for individual freedom with concern for the community welfare, and it will conceive of the community in more organic terms than the liberal was inclined to do. It will recognize that freedom from restraint is an empty kind of freedom unless that freedom is directed toward ends more ultimate than freedom itself. For freedom is not an end in itself, as the classical liberal was inclined to believe, but an essential means to the development of moral and spiritual perfection. And it loses its meaning and degenerates into license if it is not directed toward that end.

There is a truth in liberalism, according to Professor V. A. Demant, which modern liberal thought has tried to preserve without its foundations:

The truth of the liberal idea is that man cannot be confined to his political relationships. He is more than a brick in the social edifice. "The Christian Revolution" in the ancient world was an affirmation of this truth based upon the positive doctrine of man as a creature of God, with his life reaching out to an eternal world, thereby affecting his life in this. . . .

Modern liberal thought tried to preserve the truth without its foundations. It affirmed the dignity of the human person, not in the name of something larger than his social relationships would warrant, but of something smaller. It claimed liberty for the individual man, not on the ground that man is a creature with one part of his being in the eternal world, but on the ground that as a political atom he has a right to exist in himself. . . . Instead of claiming liberties *for* the pursuit of positive social purposes directed by man's spiritual relationships, it encouraged demands for liberty *from* this or that encroachment. . . .

In consequence of liberalism's emancipation from the religious basis of freedom for positive ends, the modern world has earned, not a secular freedom, but a drift towards social disintegration that is sending men in self-protection into the arms of oppressive collectivisms.

Our task is therefore to recover, in the conditions of the present world, that positively religious conception of human life that will alone save us from the consequence of the assumption that the State is the source of community instead of an instrument of it. . . . It has been for want of an organic relation between man's secular and spiritual life that the natural social functions of industry, commerce, education, family and regional politics have lost a sense of purpose. . . .

The "primacy of the spiritual" must be upheld, not as a retreat from the secular tasks of life, but as a condition of handling them aright.[10]

10. *Theology of Society* (London, 1947), pp. 64–66. Quoted with the permission of Faber and Faber.

V. Human Nature and Politics

Underlying every system of government there is some predominant conception of the nature of man and the meaning of human existence. More often than not, this idea of man is implicit rather than explicit. But if not always explicit, it is always fundamental. For what we think government can and ought to do will depend in large part upon what we think about the capacities of men and the purpose of human existence. If our conception of man's essential nature and ultimate destiny is false, i.e., unreal, we may be led to seek and apply political solutions to human and social problems that at best are useless and at worst harmful.

If we think, for example, that the evil prevalent in the world is the result of human ignorance, then we will be inclined to believe that more and better education is the remedy for it. This, indeed, was the view of the eighteenth-century French philosopher, Helvetius, who believed that education "is capable of effecting everything," it "makes us what we are," and "the virtues and vices of a nation are always necessary effects of its legislation." He believed that under a good system of education creative ability could be manufactured, since Nature "never made a dunce." Indeed, he wrote, "It is certain that great men, who now appear haphazard, will in the future be produced by the legislature, and the abilities and virtues of the citizens in great empires need not be left so much to chance: by really good education they may be infinitely multiplied."[1] The typical philosopher of

1. Quoted by Kingsley Martin, *French Liberal Thought in the Eighteenth Century* (Boston, 1929), p. 183.

the eighteenth-century Enlightenment saw no limits to the perfectibility of human nature or to man's control of nature. As man marches inexorably toward the goal of perfection on earth, through the medium of scientific discovery, even death may one day be outlawed from the universe. Is it unreasonable, Condorcet asks, "to suppose that a period must one day arrive when death will be nothing more than the effect either of extraordinary accidents, or of the slow and gradual decay of the vital powers; and that the duration of the middle space, of the interval between the birth of man and his decay, will itself have no assignable limit?"[2]

If we believe that character is primarily the product of the social environment in which the individual is reared, then, clearly, if you improve the environment, you will improve the character of men. This was the view of the nineteenth-century British Socialist, Robert Owen. "Let it not, therefore, be longer said," he wrote, "that evil or injurious actions cannot be prevented; or that the most rational habits in the rising generation cannot be universally formed. In those characters which now exhibit crime, the fault is obviously not in the individual, but the defect proceeds from the system in which the individual has been trained. Withdraw those circumstances which tend to create crime in the human character, and crime will not be created."[3]

If we are under the influence of Freudian psychology, we will be inclined to view political conflict as pathological in character and requiring the services of psychiatry to resolve it. We will be inclined to regard the view that discussion is the best means of resolving political conflict as naïve. "The time has come," says Harold D. Lasswell, "to abandon the assumption that the problem of politics is the problem of promoting discussion among all the interests concerned in a given problem. Discussion frequently complicates social difficulties, for the discussion by far-flung in-

2. *Outlines of an Historical View of the Progress of the Human Mind* (London, 1795), p. 368.

3. *A New View of Society* (1st American ed.; New York, 1825), p. 46.

terests arouses a psychology of conflict which produces obstruc-
tive, fictitious and irrelevant values. The problem of politics is
less to solve conflicts than to prevent them; less to serve as a
safety valve for social protest than to apply social energy to the
abolition of recurrent sources of strain in society."[4] "The pre-
ventive politics of the future," he says, "will be intimately allied
to general medicine, psychopathology, physiological psychology,
and related disciplines."[5]

Freedom of speech, of press, and of assembly are all designed
to promote discussion on the basis of the belief that men are
capable of rational deliberation, that they are amenable to rational
persuasion, and that discussion is a good means of resolving
conflicts over the best means of promoting the common good.
But if men, in fact, are incapable of rational deliberation; if they
are not amenable to argument; if, in fact, discussion creates more
social difficulties than it removes, then, clearly, democracy as
traditionally conceived is either a fraud or a delusion.

I

Is there a reality to which man must conform if he is to
realize fully his potentialities as a human being, or is reality a
product of human consciousness, something which men can
change and which is but a reflection of human desires? Is reality
something to which we must conform, or is it something which
we make to conform to our desires? Are there objective criteria
in terms of which we can recognize and define human nature,
or is human nature simply the reflection of prevailing social
conditions? Are moral values discovered or devised? Is justice
rooted in objective reality, or is it simply a name for what some
individuals happen to like in the way of social arrangements?
Is justice anything more than the interest of the stronger?

4. *Psychopathology and Politics* (Chicago, 1930), pp. 196–97. Quoted with
permission of the University of Chicago Press.

5. *Ibid.,* p. 203.

The answers given by intellectuals in the modern world to these questions do not follow political boundaries, but the answers have profound consequences for politics.

The notion that truth is not something to be discovered but something to be made finds explicit expression in the contemporary American climate of opinion in the philosophy of pragmatism. As William James declares: "The 'true,' to put it very briefly, is only the expedient in the way of our thinking, just as 'the right' is only the expedient in the way of our behaving."[6] Or, as he says in other words:

> Our obligation to seek truth is part of our general obligation to do what pays. The payments true ideas bring are the sole why of our duty to follow them. Identical whys exist in the case of wealth and health.[7]

> The truth of an idea is not a stagnant property inherent in it. Truth *happens* to an idea. It *becomes* true, is *made* true by events. Its verity *is* in fact an event, a process: the process namely of its verifying itself, its veri-*fication*. Its validity is the process of its valid-*ation*.[8]

An idea is true if it "works." For "ideas . . . become true just in so far as they help us to get into satisfactory relation with other parts of our experience."[9] Truth is whatever happens to be regarded as true at a particular moment and by particular individuals.

Associated with William James's conception of truth as the workability of an idea is the "will to believe." In an essay by that title he defends the thesis that "Our passional nature not only lawfully may, but must, decide an option between propositions, whenever it is a genuine option that cannot by its nature be decided on intellectual grounds."[10] By "intellectual grounds" he understood on scientific grounds—thus, he argued, when a propo-

---

6. *Pragmatism* (New York, 1928), p. 222. Quoted with the permission of Longmans, Green and Co.

7. *Ibid.*, p. 230.   8. *Ibid.*, p. 201.   9. *Ibid.*, p. 58.

10. *The Will To Believe* (New York, 1937), p. 11. Quoted with the permission of Longmans, Green and Co.

sition cannot be validated by science, we not only may but must follow the lead of our passions. In such situations, James argued, "we have the right to believe at our own risk *any* hypothesis that is live enough to tempt our will."[11] This is a more dangerous doctrine than he imagined. For although he was using it to defend our right to accept moral and religious propositions, it is a doctrine that may be used to justify believing in *anything*. If reason is powerless to guide our will or to substantiate the validity of the path taken by our will, then no standard remains by which to judge the validity of our beliefs except the emotional satisfaction which such beliefs may engender in us. This is a highly subjective standard and not a very reliable one. By subjecting truth to the domination of human desire, pragmatism would appear to be erecting "wishful thinking" into a philosophy of life. It is one thing to make our will subservient to our faith, but it is quite another thing to make our faith subservient to our will.

The greatest disciple of William James, John Dewey, abandons the word "truth" completely in favor of a conception which he calls "warranted assertability." And for the traditional search for truth he would substitute "inquiry" by the methods and with the concepts of natural science. Truth is what individuals who carry on such "inquiry" agree upon. Truth is not something which is always the same, but rather truth "evolves," and the only lasting truth is the evolutionary process. To understand this process is the task of philosophy as the handmaiden of natural science. The purpose of life is mastery over the environment. With the great advances made by the natural sciences in their control of nature, Dewey foresees man finally coming into his own as the master of his own destiny. Human nature is a reflection of social conditions. If we can learn to control those conditions, as we are learning to control them, we can mold human nature to suit our own purposes. Intelligent planning is all that is required. The failure of classical liberalism, according to Dewey, was "its failure to

11. *Ibid.*, p. 29. Italics mine.

recognize what the true and final source of change has been, and now is, the corporate intelligence embodied in science." The problem of the reconciliation of freedom and authority will be solved, Dewey thinks, only by the acceptance of the authority of science:

Neither the past nor the present affords . . . any ground for expecting that the adjustment of authority and freedom, stability and change, will be achieved by following old paths. . . . The issue, in my judgment, can be narrowed down to this question: Are there resources that have not as yet been tried out in the large field of human relations, resources that are available and that carry with them the potential promise of successful application? . . .

The resource that has not yet been tried on any large scale, in the broad field of human, social relationships is the utilization of organized intelligence, the manifold benefits and values of which we have substantial and reliable evidence in the narrower field of science.[12]

This is the gospel of social salvation by science.

Commenting upon Dewey's philosophy, the English philosopher, Bertrand Russell, has put his finger upon the most dangerous aspect of it:

His philosophy is a power philosophy, though not, like Nietzsche's, a philosophy of individual power; it is the power of the community that is felt to be valuable. It is this element of social power that seems to me to make the philosophy of instrumentalism attractive to those who are more impressed by our new control over natural forces than by the limitations to which that control is still subject. . . .

modern technique, while not altogether favorable to the lordly individual of the Renaissance, has revived the sense of the collective power of human communities. Man, formerly too humble, begins to think himself as almost a God. The Italian pragmatist Papini urges us to substitute the "Imitation of God" for the "Imitation of Christ."

In all this I feel a grave danger, the danger of what might be called cosmic impiety. The concept of "truth" as something dependent upon facts largely outside human control has been one of the ways in

12. John Dewey, "Authority and Social Change," in the Harvard Tercentenary publication, *Authority and the Individual* (Cambridge, 1937), pp. 183–84. Quoted with the permission of the Harvard University Press.

which philosophy hitherto has inculcated the necessary element of humility. When this check upon pride is removed, a further step is taken on the road towards a certain kind of madness—the intoxication of power . . . to which modern men, whether philosophers or not, are prone. I am persuaded that this intoxication is the greatest danger of our time, and that any philosophy which, however unintentionally, contributes to it is increasing the danger of vast social disaster.[13]

If Bertrand Russell, who is known to be a skeptic in religious matters, sees grave danger in the substitution of the "Imitation of God" for the "Imitation of Christ," his testimony should be all the more convincing to those who would reject a Christian's warning as a partisan complaint. It is what Russell calls "cosmic impiety" that is characteristic of much modern thinking and its most dangerous aspect.

Translated into political terms, the issue is this: Does the state arise out of natural necessity and continue in existence in order that men might be helped by its institutions to realize their inherent potentialities as persons? Or is the state an instrumentality of human will, to be used in any fashion which those in control of the state deem desirable? Is there something inherent in human nature which demands the state and defines and limits its function, or is the state simply a conventional and arbitrary instrument of human will? Is the task of politics fundamentally technological or moral? The answer to that question depends upon the way in which we answer this further question: Is human nature part of a reality which includes but transcends nature, or is human nature the product and reflection of prevailing social conditions? Is man created in the image of God, or is human nature simply the reflection of social conditions? Is history, as Marx believed, "the activity of man pursuing his own aims," or is history a dialogue between God and man?

The prevailing view in modern culture appears to be that

13. *A History of Western Philosophy* (New York, 1945), pp. 827–28. Copyright, 1945, by Bertrand Russell. Published by Simon and Schuster, Inc. Quoted by permission of Simon and Schuster, Inc.

history is simply the activity of man pursuing his own aims and that human nature is nothing more than the reflection of social conditions at any given time. Change those social conditions, many modern intellectuals tell us, and you can change human nature. There is no limit to what "organized intelligence," in Dewey's phrase, can do to make human nature over. It is not a belief peculiar to liberalism, communism, socialism, or fascism but is held by them all; indeed, it appears to be a self-evident presupposition of most modern thought. Fascinated by the apparent mastery of nature by natural science, many moderns would like to extend that mastery to human nature itself.

These would-be molders of "human nature" are especially prominent among those who call themselves "social scientists." A prominent social psychologist, Professor Hadley Cantril, expresses an idea which one encounters frequently among social scientists when he says:

> We can say, then, that there is nothing fixed, or static, or immutable about human nature. We can say that there is no one single accurate characterization of it. We can say that it is fluid, constantly changing, that occasionally, under a new set of conditions, it exhibits new and heretofore undreamed-of possibilities. When conditions are changed, human nature is changed.
>
> Human nature as it characterizes any group at any given time is what it is because of the conditions under which the individuals in that group have matured. And the only way to bring about the human nature we want is to plan scientifically the kind of social and economic environment offering the best conditions for the development of human nature in the direction we would specify—a direction that spells freedom from group conflict and freedom for personal development.[14]

So commonplace is this kind of statement today that few would think of challenging it, and not many would find anything particularly dangerous in it. And I am sure that those who utter

14. "Don't Blame It on Human Nature," *New York Times Magazine*, July 6, 1947. Quoted with permission of the *New York Times*.

such statements would be the most surprised of all if it were suggested to them that they were promoting an idea that could have pernicious practical consequences. I do not question the nobility of the sentiments of the social scientists who propound this doctrine, but I would point out that there is a logical hiatus in their reasoning and dangerous practical, political consequences which that reasoning obscures even from themselves.

You cannot both deny the existence of a personality which is anything more than a reflection of social conditions and at the same time affirm the desirability of developing a personality which is independent of social conditioning. If human nature is but a reflection of social conditions, if there is no single accurate characterization of it, if there is nothing immutable in human nature, then there is nothing in "human nature" that can possibly serve as a standard with which to measure "freedom for personal development." In the last analysis, what constitutes "personal development" will be decided upon by those who undertake "to plan scientifically" the social conditions most conducive to *their* conception of what human nature should be. Indeed, Cantril speaks of bringing about the human nature "we want" and of directing the "development of human nature" along the lines "we would specify." If our political task is conceived as bringing about "the human nature we want," our guide in deciding what we shall do, how we shall plan, will not be human nature but the will of those who are doing the planning. One might well ask at this point if it is not a reflection of that "cosmic impiety" of which Bertrand Russell speaks to assert that the direction in which human nature should be developed is wholly within our power "to specify." Are we not, perhaps, ascribing to ourselves powers which we do not possess and which it would be not only impious but dangerous to usurp?

But what, precisely, it might be asked, is the danger in the extension of the scientific mastery of nature to the scientific conquest of human nature itself? The danger is the tyranny of the conditioners over the conditioned. "For the power of Man to make himself what he pleases means . . . [ultimately] the power of some men to make other men what *they* please."[15] The motives of the would-be molders of human nature in the democratic states may be, and probably are, purer and nobler than the motives that animate the Fascists and the Communists, but the end-result is likely to be the same—the enslavement of the many to the capricious wills of the few. The good of humanity would be their slogan, but the definition of that good would be their own.

But why should we assume that the motives of the would-be molders of human nature should be so bad? Why can we not expect them to be restrained by the dictates of conscience and to do that which is good for the human race? We cannot assume that they will be restrained by the dictates of conscience, since what conscience dictates will be precisely what they shall decide. We cannot assume that they will be guided by some objective standard of what is good for the human race, since what is good for the human race is precisely what they shall be called upon to decide. The conditioners will be beyond good and evil, since what good and evil are to mean is precisely what they shall decide. C. S. Lewis has probably seen and pointed out the consequences of such thinking more clearly than anyone else, and speaking of these would-be molders of human nature, he says:

. . . at first they may look upon themselves as servants and guardians of humanity and conceive that they have a "duty" to do it "good." But it is only by confusion that they can remain in this state. They recognize the concept of duty as the result of certain processes which they can now control. Their victory has consisted precisely in emerging from the state in which they were acted upon by those processes to the state in which they use them as tools. One of the things they now have to decide is whether they will, or will not, so condition the rest of us that we can go on having the old idea of duty and the old reac-

15. C. S. Lewis, *The Abolition of Man* (New York, 1947), p. 37. Copyrighted 1947 by the Macmillan Company and used with the Macmillan Company's permission.

tions to it. How can duty help them to decide that? Duty itself is up for trial: it cannot also be the judge. And "good" fares no better. They know quite well how to produce a dozen different conceptions of good in us. The question is which, if any, they should produce. No conception of good can help them to decide. It is absurd to fix on one of the things they are comparing and make it the standard of comparison.

To some it will appear that I am inventing a factitious difficulty for my Conditioners. Other, more simple-minded, critics may ask "Why should you suppose they will be such bad men?" But I am not supposing them to be bad men. They are, rather, not men (in the old sense) at all. They are, if you like, men who have sacrificed their own share in traditional humanity in order to devote themselves to the task of deciding what "Humanity" shall henceforth mean. "Good" and "bad" applied to them are words without content: for it is from them that the content of these words is henceforward to be derived. . . . It is not that they are bad men. They are not men at all. Stepping outside the *Tao*, they have stepped into the void. Nor are their subjects necessarily unhappy men. They are not men at all: they are artefacts. Man's final conquest has proved to be the abolition of Man.[16]

Men are conceived no longer as personalities to be preserved, but as things to be manipulated. Politics is conceived as a science of social perfection, a kind of social engineering. And this conception of politics finds its culmination in the totalitarian dictatorship.

II

Opposed to this way of thinking is the wisdom embodied in the Hebraic-Greek-Christian tradition, and is it only through the recovery of the teaching of that tradition, in my opinion, that democracy, and, indeed, the humanity of man, can be preserved. What does that tradition teach us? Among other things, it teaches us that reality is not something men make but something to which they must conform. Man is not his own maker but a being

16. *Ibid.*, pp. 39–41. Copyrighted 1947 by the Macmillan Company and used with the Macmillan Company's permission.

created in the image and likeness of God. His nature is not something he makes, or something that is shaped by social conditions, but something he is given. Man is conscious not only of what he is but of what he ought to be and may become. And the perfection of his nature, of what he ought to be and hence essentially is, is the purpose of his existence. Man does not belong to himself but to God who created him. History, therefore, is not, as Marx declared it to be, "the activity of man pursuing his own aims" but rather a dialogue between God and man, with God taking the initiative and man either fleeing or responding to His call. The essential meaning of history is the restoration of personality through redemption from evil. And the evil from which men need to be redeemed is the evil which is manifested in pride, avarice, envy, anger, greed, lust, and sloth.

There is a sense in which human nature can change—indeed, must change—if man is to realize fully the potentialities of his humanity; but this change does not take place in accordance with someone's arbitrary conception of what a good human nature would be like but in accordance with the laws of its own being. And that change is dictated less by the social conditions under which men live than it is by the spiritual and moral response which they make to those conditions. There is a sense in which, as A. E. Taylor has pointed out, the ideal of Socrates and the Christian ideal are essentially identical:

The central thought in both cases is that man is born a creature of temporality and mutability into a temporal and mutable environment. But, in virtue of the fact that there is something "divine" in him, he cannot but aspire to a good which is above time and mutability, and thus the right life is, from first to last, a process by which the merely secular and temporal self is re-made in the likeness of the eternal. . . . The thought is that the real nature of the soul has to be learned from a consideration of the nature of the specific "good" to which it aspires. A creature whose well-being consists in living for an "eternal" good cannot be a mere thing of time and change.[17]

17. *Plato: The Man and His Work* (New York, 1929), p. 192. Quoted with permission of the Dial Press.

In the Christian tradition this remaking of the secular and temporal self in the likeness of the eternal is effected by the grace of God in Christ, i.e., by the power and pardon of God. It requires repentance on the part of the individual and a reorientation of his thoughts and actions from self to God. It requires the submission of his will to the will and purpose of God. This submission does not destroy his nature but perfects it. The process of perfection is a continuous one and is rarely, if ever, completed in this life. The church exists as the principal institution through which the grace of God is mediated to man, and the usual means for the transmission of grace are the sacraments and the Holy Scripture. The "remaking" of human nature, then, is not a political task but a spiritual one, the responsibility not of the state but of the church.

The Hebraic-Greek-Christian tradition also teaches us that one of the distinctive characteristics of man is his rationality. Man is defined in the classical tradition as a rational animal. This definition does not mean that man is the most rational or intelligent of all animals but rather that he is a unique being. It is not reason engrafted upon animality that describes man best but rather reason informing and transfiguring animality. It is not that emasculated idea of reason which has infected post-Cartesian philosophy, a reason cut loose from love and debarred from vision, which the definition of man as a rational animal implies but rather a reason directed toward God as its ultimate goal. It has been said that "Reason is like a light which by its own inner force can move nowhere. It must be carried in order to move."[18] And many modern thinkers insist that it is carried by the irrational forces of interest and emotion. But the passion which carries reason and focuses its attention may not always be a blind passion but may be a seeing passion; and in the Christian tradition this seeing passion is the love of God. Man is not only a rational animal but a passionate one. All of us are moved by passion. The question is: Will it be a

18. Hans J. Morgenthau, *Scientific Man vs. Power Politics* (Chicago, 1946), p. 155.

passion for good or for evil, a passion that enslaves or liberates us? In the Christian tradition the integrity of man's rationality is secured by the belief that, through reason directed by the love of God, men may be brought closer to God. St. Anselm declared: "That the rational creature has been created just by God in order to be happy through enjoying him—this should not be doubted. For that purpose namely is man rational that he distinguish between just and unjust, good and evil, the greater and the lesser good. Otherwise he would have been created in vain."

The Hebraic-Greek-Christian tradition also teaches us that man is a creature of free will. Man is distinguished from other living things not only by virtue of his rationality but by virtue of his freedom of choice. Only man is conscious of the problem of morality, since only he is conscious of a discrepancy between what he is and what he ought to be. He is free to choose between alternative forms of action as well as to deliberate upon that choice. He is free to choose that course of action dictated by rational deliberation which will lead to the perfection of his nature or to reject it. If the course of action he chooses enables him to become a better man, we call that action good, if a worse man, bad. And it is this freedom to will the good or the bad that is the source both of man's greatness and of his degradation. The tragedy of human existence is man's proneness to choose the evil way rather than the good. The defect lies, however, not so much in man's incapacity to know the good as in his unwillingness to act upon it when known.

The Hebraic-Greek-Christian tradition teaches us, in short, that the ultimate reality behind nature and history is a creative, rational, moral, loving Will and that man, since he is created in the image and likeness of God, achieves the perfection of his being in willing submission to the Reason and Will of Him that governs the universe. Men may resist that will or submit to it, but they cannot change it. The ultimate reality cannot be made over to conform to our desires—it is not something we can make or manipulate but something to which ultimately we must conform. Ultimately, all our actions will be judged by a standard which is not our own but God's.

Though limited and conditioned by the social environment, man is free to transcend the natural and historical process in which he is involved; and it is this freedom which accounts both for his creative and for his destructive potentialities. It is the transcendence of man's spirit over the physical, natural, and historical processes which distinguishes man from the beast, and it is for this reason that human nature can never be completely comprehended or explained in physical, natural, or historical terms. The sex impulse, for example, which man shares with the animals, is never so purely biological in man as it is in the beast. For, with man, sex is bound up with love; and when man endeavors to make the sexual act a purely physical thing, it is only by an act of perversion that he is able to do so.[19] Only man is capable of perverting his natural impulses, animals are not. The same thing is true of man's economic desires. They, too, are never purely physical but have a spiritual dimension. Reinhold Niebuhr pointed this out very well when he said:

Economic desires are never merely the expression of the hunger or the survival impulse in human life. The desires for "power and glory" are subtly compounded with the more primeval impulse. The

19. Plato describes love as the desire of the soul for the good apprehended as beauty. Love is not of the flesh primarily or of individual persons, but it is an attraction to perfection. Plato would agree with Freud that love is the root impulse of life; but, whereas Freud would describe all idealistic impulses as sublimations of physical desire, Plato would represent physical desire as a distorted manifestation of a spiritual impulse. Now, as Raphael Demos has pointed out, "if it is legitimate for Freud to go behind the apparent content of an impulse, so it is for Plato; and the question whether the 'lower' or the 'higher' impulses should be taken as fundamental cannot be settled except by reference to a general metaphysical standpoint." If perfection, as Plato believed, "is the principle of reality," then "to desire an object is to desire the good" (*Plato: Selections* [New York, 1927], Introduction, p. xxiii). Quoted with permission of Charles Scribner's Sons.

lion's desire for food is satisfied when his maw is crammed. Man's desire for food is more easily limited than other human desires; yet the hunger impulse is subject to endless refinements and perversions of the gourmand. Shelter and raiment have much more extensible limits than food. Man's coat is never merely a cloak for his nakedness but the badge of his vocation, or the expression of an artistic impulse, or a method of attracting the other sex, or a proof of social position. Man's house is not merely his shelter but, even more than his raiment, the expression of his personality, and the symbol of his power, position and prestige.[20]

"For better or for worse," as Helmut Kuhn has said, man "is an altogether unique being, projecting, as it were, into a dimension foreign to animality."[21]

III

What, then, is the science of politics? Is it a science like physics, a science like engineering, or what?

Now physics is a science which deals with things which cannot possibly be otherwise than they are. It is concerned with relations which are entirely independent of human volition. It is a search for *necessary* relations. But, because political science deals with the behavior of human beings, it is not a science of that kind. Because man is able both to choose between alternative ways of acting and to deliberate upon that choice, the behavior of human beings is never as predictable as is the behavior of atoms. As a consequence, political science is concerned not with that which is absolutely necessary but with that which is contingent. It deals with things which may be other than they are. And for that reason it is not a speculative science but a practical one.

Because it is a practical science, political science is more like engineering than it is like physics. The physicist is interested in

20. *The Children of Light and the Children of Darkness* (New York, 1944), pp. 61–62. Quoted with permission of Charles Scribner's Sons.

21. "Philosophy and Religion: The Humanity of Man," in *A State University Surveys the Humanities* (Chapel Hill, 1945), p. 75.

discovering the physical laws of the universe for their own sake. Whether his discoveries have any practical significance is not his concern. But the practical application of the principles discovered by physics is the peculiar concern of the engineer. The engineer is not interested in the principles of physics for their own sake but in order that he may design and construct bridges—not bridges in the abstract but particular bridges at particular places. Obviously, he must know something about the principles of physics if the bridges he builds are not to collapse, but he does not need to know so much about these principles as the physicist does or to know them in exactly the same way. What he needs is a practical knowledge, a working knowledge, of these principles, just as a carpenter needs a working knowledge of mathematics.

Political science is like engineering, in that it is a practical science. It is interested in knowledge not for the sake of knowledge but for the sake of action. The action at which politics aims is policy and, more specifically, legislation, since it is through legislation that policy takes shape and form and the coercive power of the state is put behind it. But although both engineering and political science are practical sciences, although both can be distinguished from theoretical sciences like physics, there is a significant difference between them. For the one is concerned with *doing* something, and the other is concerned with *making* something.

The objects with which the engineer deals are inanimate, material things (bricks, steel, concrete, etc.), and the engineer is concerned with shaping or making those things into useful objects, such as buildings, highways, and bridges. The materials are transformed by the engineer in conformity with some useful purpose which he has in mind. The purpose does not inhere in the things themselves but in the mind of the engineer. Engineering is a science of making things, a productive science or technology. The products of technology may be used for good purposes or bad, but, once made, the technician's task is completed.

The objects with which engineering deals are inanimate, material things, but the objects with which politics is concerned are human beings—human beings who are not things but personalities. The attempt to manipulate human beings like material things is destructive of their very essence. Human beings are not like so many bricks or pieces of steel that have only to be laid in the right place according to a blueprint. They can co-operate or rebel, and it is only by enlisting their co-operation that the purpose of politics can be achieved.

Politics differs from engineering in that it is concerned with doing something rather than with making something. Politics is concerned with action, not with construction. Politics, moreover, comes into being in order to assist men in doing what men are already naturally predisposed to do. Man is by nature a social being. He requires the fellowship and services of other men. He does not create society but is born into it. He does not choose to live in society but lives in society of necessity. Steel does not have to be made into bridges; it has no inherent predispositon to *be* anything—it can be manipulated and used in any fashion the engineer decides is appropriate to his purpose. But human beings, unlike steel, embody ends in themselves; they are predisposed to live in society. Men, moreover, are not content simply to exist. It is not life alone that they desire, but a good life. And it is the function of politics to assist men in achieving this good life in society.

For these reasons political science is more like the physician's art than it is like the science of engineering. The normal body of the human organism naturally tends toward health. When the body becomes diseased or disordered, medical therapy consists in trying to help the organism to cure itself, to assist nature in doing what nature is already predisposed to do. The physician ministers to an end which nature itself pursues. So political science ministers to an end which is not of its own devising but which is inherent in life itself. It comes into being in order to help men live a good life in society. It does not invent that end but finds that end inherent in all human striving. The task of the statesman, therefore, is more like the task of the physician than it is like the task of the engineer. It is practical wisdom rather than productive knowledge that the statesman needs. The statesman is not concerned with making anything but rather with inspiring right action, and his ability to inspire right action is the measure of his statesmanship. It is not, then, a question of bringing about "the human nature we want" and of planning scientifically "for the development of human nature in the direction we would specify" but rather a question of discovering those principles of conduct which will promote the perfection of human nature and of providing a social environment congenial to the realization of those principles in practice. It is not so much a matter of imposing something upon men as it is of releasing the creative forces for good already in men and of restraining that which is bad. In short, politics is not a kind of technology but a form of moral endeavor.

The state is not a contrivance to be used by the individuals who happen to control it for purposes which they elect but has its origin in the rational and social nature of man. Its purpose is dictated not by the subjective desires of particular individuals but by the nature of man and the end for which he is destined. The state exists to promote justice among men, to help men to become better human beings, to unleash their creative capacities for good, and to restrain their propensity to do evil. This justice is not a subjective concept but is rooted in objective reality. A just society would be one in which each individual was enabled to perform that social function for which he is best fitted by virtue and capacity and was rewarded in proportion to his contribution. In his controversy with the Sophists, Plato argued— and I think successfully—that restraint is necessary for the per-

VI.   The Moral Foundation of Democracy

There is no more vivid description of the transition from democracy to tyranny than that contained in the eighth book of Plato's *Republic*. Reading it today, we are impressed with its striking relevance to the contemporary political scene, and there is no greater tribute to the enduring wisdom of Plato than that fact. That Plato himself was not attached to democracy as a form of government does not lessen the relevance of his analysis. If we mean by democracy the unrestrained rule of the many in their own interest, then this was a form of government regarded as perverted not only by Plato and Aristotle but by the framers of our own Constitution. The constitutional, representative democracy which the framers of our Constitution established bears considerable resemblance to that form of government which Aristotle described as a "polity" and which he regarded as the best practicable of all constitutions.

I

The transition from democracy to tyranny is described by Plato as a process of both individual and social disintegration, and the latter is depicted as having its roots in the former. When the individual revolts against tradition and authority, when instinct and desire are exalted above reason, when intellect is subordinated to will, when all desires become lawful and no standard is left for choosing among them, then at last a master-passion, "as leader of the soul, takes madness for the captain of its guard and breaks out in frenzy; if it can lay hold upon any thoughts or desires that are of good report and still capable of shame, it kills them or drives them forth, until it has purged the soul of all sobriety and called in the partisans of madness to fill the vacant place."[1] And just as a single tyrant desire takes possession of the individual who knows no restraints, so the mass of individuals in a society that knows no restraints at last submit their wills to the will of a tyrant, in order that they might escape the tyranny of their own passions. Freedom, now having become license, becomes an intolerable burden, and they seek to escape from it by submission to the tyrant. Erich Fromm has described this escape from freedom in modern psychological terms; but the more profound analysis was suggested by Plato five centuries before Christ. There is no more accurate description of Hitler and his kind than Plato's description of the despotic man who, like a lunatic, "dreams that he can lord it over all mankind and heaven besides." For "when nature or habit or both have combined the traits of drunkenness, lust, and lunacy, then you have the perfect specimen of the despotic man."[2]

The despotic man and the despotic state are but the end-products of a progressive degeneration that begins when ambition usurps the rule of reason. At first, ambition is motivated by a love of honor and is an ambition to serve. This honorable ambition gives way in time to the passion for wealth. From a means to life, wealth increasingly becomes the end of life. At first, the passion for wealth holds the appetitive desires in check; but to the extent that it encourages the luxurious indulgence of the body, to the extent that the many are pauperized to satisfy the insatiable cravings of the few, the appetitive desires are increasingly "liberated" from restraint, and anarchy in the soul and society is the result. The man who is "under the sway of a host of unnecessary pleasures and appetites" replaces the "miserly oligarch" as the

1. *The Republic of Plato*, trans. F. M. Cornford (London, 1945), p. 298. Quoted with permission of the Oxford University Press.

2. *Ibid.*, p. 298.

dominant type of man in society. "His life is subject to no order or restraint," and freedom comes to mean to do as one pleases. The parent falls into the habit of behaving like the child, the father is afraid of his sons, and children have neither fear nor respect for their parents. The teacher flatters his pupils, and the pupils repay the flattery with contempt. Family bonds are loosened, and promiscuous sexual indulgence replaces marital fidelity. "The citizens become so sensitive that they resent the slightest application of control as intolerable tyranny, and in their resolve to have no master they end by disregarding even the law, written or unwritten."[3]

Bred by the spirit of license, a class of drones emerges which takes possession of political offices, intent upon nothing more than occupying them for their own advantage. At the same time, another class is steadily bent upon the amassing of wealth. And it is this class which provides provender for the drones. A third class, the largest of all, is composed of the people with few possessions and little or no interest in politics. The plundered rich, in an effort to protect their wealth from the drones, become more and more reactionary. Eventually, in an effort to protect themselves from both the drones and the reactionary rich, the people put forward a single champion of their interests.

"In the early days he has a smile and a greeting for everyone he meets; disclaims any absolute power; makes large promises to his friends and to the public; sets about the relief of debtors and the distribution of the land to the people and to his supporters."[4] But soon the people's champion begins to act more and more like a despot. "If he suspects some of cherishing thoughts of freedom and not submitting to his rule," he finds pretexts for doing away with them. He requests a private army to protect him from the enemies of the people; but what is first looked upon as a popular militia to protect the people's interests gradually turns

3. *Ibid.*, p. 289.   4. *Ibid.*, p. 293.

into a weapon with which to exploit the people and keep them in bondage. "The bolder spirits among those who have helped him to power and now hold positions of influence will begin to speak their mind of him and among themselves to criticize his policy. If the despot is to maintain his rule, he must gradually make away with all these malcontents, until he has not a friend or an enemy left who is of any account."[5] The best elements in society are purged until all who are courageous, high-minded, and intelligent are either killed or silenced. "The people . . . have escaped the smoke only to fall into the fire, exchanging service to free men for the tyranny of slaves. That freedom which knew no bounds must now put on the livery of the most harsh and bitter servitude, where the slave has become the master."[6] Freedom conceived as license leads to anarchy, and anarchy manifests itself politically in tyranny.

II

True freedom requires both knowledge of the good and the will to choose the good when known. The denial of either is a denial of freedom, and the denial of freedom is the rejection of that moral agency in man which characterizes his humanity. In one of the best analyses of the rise of National Socialism in Germany, Helmut Kuhn explains the acceptance of Hitler as being made possible by a "flight from freedom into forgetfulness." "Freedom," he says, "is rational choice."

The flight from freedom into forgetfulness presented itself, within the rarefied atmosphere of abstract thought, as a dialectic through

5. *Ibid.*, p. 293.

6. *Ibid.*, p. 296. A great deal of nonsense is written about Plato today, and much of his thinking is presented in a distorted form to modern readers. A recent example of this kind of distortion is K. R. Popper's *The Open Society and Its Enemies* (London, 1945). An excellent answer to Popper's arguments will be found in Robert Jordan's "The Revolt against Philosophy: The Spell of Popper," in John Wild (ed.), *The Return to Reason* (Chicago, 1953), and in John Wild's *Plato's Modern Enemies and the Theory of Natural Law* (Chicago, 1953).

which Reason was divorced from Choice. The Historicist, fastening on understanding to the exclusion of choice, reduced the mind to an impotent spectator. The Existentialist, exalting choice at the expense of reason, entrusted the self with a blind power of decision, thus reducing it to an irresponsible agent. After whittling away freedom from both ends, the two found themselves united in the task of consecrating the unfreedom of the totalitarian state. A pre-established harmony obtained between their joint teaching on the one hand and the behavior which the Third Reich expected from its citizens on the other. The required attitude combined the passivity of the spectator with the blind spontaneity of the unreasoning agent.[7]

The preservation of freedom demands that we recover our faith both in the ability of man to know the good and in his capacity, within the limitations of historical conditioning and the defectiveness of his will, to choose the good when known. That he will inevitably fall short of knowing the good in its completeness and of acting upon it unselfishly in every instance—so much we must concede to the intellectual and moral frailty of human nature—but only in the ever constant effort to transcend his limitations with the help of God can man's freedom be preserved and enlarged. When we talk today about the preservation of democracy, what most of us, I think, are concerned about is the preservation of freedom. We realize that democratic forms and institutions find their essential and ultimate meaning in the preservation and enlargement of human freedom. They are not ends in themselves but means to an ultimate end. They are not identical with freedom but the means through which freedom may find its best political expression.

Plato believed that in the ideal state political power and love of the good would be combined in the same individuals. This is the essential meaning of his declaration that in the ideal state philosophers will be kings, and kings philosophers. He meant by "philosophers" lovers of wisdom, seekers after the good. Whereas

7. *Freedom: Forgotten and Remembered* (Chapel Hill, 1943), p. 25. Quoted with permission of the University of North Carolina Press.

Plato, however, believed that only a few members of society could ever aspire to a life of virtue, it is the faith underlying modern democracy that all men may aspire to that life of virtue which Plato would restrict to the few.

That faith has a long and ancient lineage. It is probably first suggested by the Stoics and finds explicit expression in the writings of Cicero. "There is no human being of any race," writes Cicero, "who, if he finds a guide, cannot attain to virtue."[8] Men, he argues, are more alike than they are different, and between man and man there is no difference in kind. The distinguishing characteristic of man is his ability to reason, and it is this reason which links one man to another. Men attain virtue by following the principles of that law which "the gods have given to the human race." "Law is not a product of human thought, nor is it any enactment of peoples, but something eternal which rules the whole universe by its wisdom in command and prohibition. . . . Law is the primal and ultimate mind of God whose reason directs all things either by compulsion or restraint."[9] In a celebrated passage in the *Republic*, Cicero declares:

. . . True law is right reason in agreement with nature; it is of universal application, unchanging and everlasting; it summons to duty by its commands, and averts from wrongdoing by its prohibitions. And it does not lay its commands or prohibitions upon good men in vain, though neither have any effect on the wicked. It is a sin to try to alter this law, nor is it allowable to attempt to repeal any part of it, and it is impossible to abolish it entirely. We cannot be freed from its obligations by senate or people, and we need not look outside ourselves for an expounder or interpreter of it. And there will not be different laws at Rome and at Athens, or different laws now and in the future, but one eternal and unchangeable law will be valid for all nations and all times, and there will be one master and ruler, that is, God, over us all, for he is the author of this law, its promulgator and its enforcing judge. Whoever is disobedient is fleeing from himself

8. *Laws* i. 10. 30, trans. Clinton W. Keyes (Loeb ed.; London, 1928).

9. *Ibid.* ii. 4. 8.

and denying his human nature, and by reason of this very fact he will suffer the worst penalties, even if he escapes what is commonly considered punishment.[10]

It is in the light of this law that all men are equal—equal not in wealth, in talents, in physical strength or learning but equal in the capacity to distinguish justice from injustice, right from wrong. And it is this capacity, guided by the law of nature, that makes possible to all men equally the life of virtue which Plato thought possible only for the few. And it is these two doctrines—the doctrine of natural law and the equality of men—which lie at the foundation of what today we call "democracy" and which sharply distinguish it from the totalitarian systems.

The Stoic conception of natural law is transmitted to the Middle Ages and from the Middle Ages to modern times through the teachings of Christianity, which retain the Stoic conception but identify it more explicitly as an expression of the eternal law of God. Christianity also teaches that a portion of that eternal law is revealed to men directly by God in the Divine Law, which both confirms and supplements the natural law of reason. This Divine Law is revealed in the Old Testament in the Ten Commandments which God gave to Moses and in the New by the commandment of Christ that we should love one another. The commandment that we should love one another does not abrogate the injunction of the natural law that we should render unto each man his due, but goes beyond it. And there is ascribed to the natural law a function not clearly perceived by the Stoics, namely, preparation through a life of virtue for a life eternal.

While the Stoic proclamation of a natural law emphasized the capacity of men to distinguish right from wrong, it also had the practical effect of emphasizing the inability of men to attain moral perfection through their own efforts. And men found themselves crying out in despair with Paul: "The good that I would, I do not, but the evil which I would not, that I do." And Christianity

10. *Republic* iii. 22, trans. Clinton W. Keyes (Loeb ed.; London, 1928).

taught men that only through the love of God, through the reorientation of one's thoughts and actions from self to God, through the submission of one's will to the will of God, could one hope to fulfil the law of God in its completeness. This is what Augustine meant when he said: "The law was therefore given, in order that grace might be sought; grace was given, in order that the law might be fulfilled."[11] And, again, "Our will is by the law shown to be weak, that grace may heal its infirmity."[12] Where Augustine, however, tended to emphasize the great disparity between nature and grace, later Christian thinkers, and notably Thomas Aquinas, argued that "grace does not annul nature but perfects it." The defect of man lies not in his reason but in his will.

Christianity does not deny the wisdom of the Stoics but incorporates it in its own teaching and adds to it. Augustine points out that man is not simply a citizen of this world but a pilgrim seeking the Kingdom of God. "Two cities," he says, "have been formed by two loves: the earthly by the love of self, even to the contempt of God; the heavenly by the love of God, even to the contempt of self . . . the one seeks glory from men; but the greatest glory of the other is God, the witness of conscience."[13] The Kingdom of God is above all states, races, and classes and knows neither free man nor slave, Gentile nor Jew, male nor female. It is a universal community of persons bound together by mutual love and the love of God. The Stoic conception of equality is not denied but is given a spiritual content and meaning which it lacked. Absolute justice and perfect peace are found only in this kingdom, where love rules supreme. All earthly kingdoms, due to the defective will of man, necessarily fall short of this perfection. The peace and justice at which earthly king-

11. *On the Spirit and the Letter*, Book XXXIV, in Whitney I. Oates (ed.), *Basic Writings of Saint Augustine* (2 vols.; New York, 1948), I, 487.

12. *Ibid*. Book XV, in Oates, *op. cit.*, I, 472.

13. *City of God* xiv. 28, in Oates, *op. cit.*, II, 274.

doms aim are good but only relatively good, for the peace and justice at which they aim, while essential to the attainment of everlasting peace and perfect justice, are not identical with them. Men owe allegiance to civil society; but, because they have an ultimate destiny that transcends life on earth, they have a greater obligation and a greater allegiance, namely, an allegiance to God.

The effect of this teaching is not only to distinguish the secular from the spiritual spheres but to place the secular authority under the sanction of a higher authority. And the life of wisdom and virtue, which Plato thought possible only for a few, is now conceived as being available through the grace of God to all men equally. And this has important consequences for politics. For if there is an authority higher than the authority of any particular state, then no state can demand our absolute obedience or attempt to control every aspect of our lives. This is the issue which sharply separates the totalitarian states in the modern world from the democracies. The totalitarian state is made possible only by the denial of a higher allegiance, and its totalitarian character arises from a refusal to acknowledge the existence of a sphere of human life over which no political control may legitimately be exercised. Democracies recognize that there are aspects of human life which the state may not legitimately control; and that recognition has its roots, when it is recognized, in the teachings of the Christian religion. Above the authority of the state, there is the authority of God, and this is precisely what the totalitarian states refuse to acknowledge. The authority of God may be conceived as mediated by the church or as communicated directly to the private conscience of the individual; but the form in which the authority of God is recognized is less important than is the recognition of that authority itself.

Freedom and authority are often thought of today as being in opposition to one another, and we frequently hear the modern dictatorships referred to as "authoritarian." Now authority means the right to enforce obedience, but it is precisely the unwillingness of dictators like Hitler and Stalin to feel any necessity for justifying their power that is characteristic of their rule. They deny that anyone may question their right to rule, indeed, deny that there is any authority or any standard of right in terms of which their actions may be evaluated.

The totalitarian dictatorship is the embodiment not of authority but of naked power—it repudiates the demands of reason, justice, and God. It is an effort to fill the void left by the repudiation of reason and of God by a will that is unguided by reason, unrestrained by considerations of justice, and unmindful of the commandments of God. It is not government in the true sense of the word but a perverted attempt to employ the techniques of government when government fails. The total character of the dictatorship is necessitated by the *lack* of any common authority. Compulsion replaces consent in every sphere of life, because there is no longer any common agreement obliging consent in any sphere. No authority exists to which an appeal can be taken. The will of the tyrant is the final court of appeal, and that will is a purely arbitrary one. It is useless to appeal to the tyrant's reason or sense of justice, for the tyrant denies that he must justify his actions in terms of reason or of justice. It is enough that he has commanded an action—the rightfulness of his command is not subject to debate, and it may not be questioned. And it was the positivist jurists who proclaimed that law is nothing but the will of the ruling power who prepared the way for this tyranny. Emil Brunner has said: "The totalitarian state is simply and solely legal positivism in political practice, the abrogation in actual fact of the classical and Christian idea of a divine 'law of nature.' . . . If there is no justice transcending the state, then the state can declare anything it likes to be law; there is no limit set to its arbitrariness save its actual power to give force to its will. If it does so in the form of a logically coherent system, it thereby fulfills the one condition to which the legality of law is bound in the formalistic view of law. The totalitarian state is the inevitable result of the slow disintegration of the idea of justice in the Western world." The totalitarian state, Brunner points out, is not a criminal conspiracy but the product of the Western world's own thinking, "the ineluctable consequence of its own positivism, a positivism void of faith and inimical to metaphysics and religion."[14]

It is not a characteristic feature of democracy that it dispenses with authority; that is, instead, characteristic of tyranny. There can be no freedom without authority, for without authority freedom degenerates into license. The state of anarchy which Plato describes as preceding the rise of tyranny is characterized by the lack of any order in individual and social life, by the lack

14. *Justice and the Social Order* (New York: Harper & Bros., 1945), pp. 7–8. Brunner describes the disintegration of the idea of justice in this way: "Its disintegration set in with the Age of Reason. Firstly, the *divine* law of nature, the objective, super-human standard of justice, became the subjective law of human reason, its substance soon being narrowed down into the individualistic notion of subjective rights of man. Later, following the trend of the time, the element of 'nature' in law was reinterpreted in a naturalistic sense. The historicism of the Romantic period then declared war on a timelessly valid justice, replacing it by the conception of justice as a historical growth. It was, however, the positivism of the nineteenth century, with its denial of the metaphysical and superhuman, which dissolved the idea of justice by proclaiming the relativity of all views of justice. Thereby the idea of justice was stripped of all divine dignity and law abandoned to the vagaries of human will. The view that justice is of its nature relative became the dogma of the jurists, and the proof seemed to lie at hand in the concrete facts of history. Men ceased to believe in an eternal standard of justice transcending all human legislation; the difference between right and wrong became a convention, law was conceived as the mere product of the reigning power. Finally the idea of justice was reduced to a mere husk by the complete codification of law at the beginning of the nineteenth century, after which it meant nothing more than the demand for a system of law without contradiction in form, but without any value as a criterion in substance.

"Hence it was only to be expected that one day a political power devoid of all religious scruples should discard the last vestiges of the traditional idea of justice and proclaim the will of the ruling power as the sole canon of appeal in matters of law" (*ibid.*, pp. 6–7). Quoted with permission of Harper and Brothers.

onal restraint. And it is within the framework of rational
nt that the democratic principle of majority rule is to be
........stood.

III

It is an accepted and distinguishing principle of democratic
government that, as John Locke put it, "the majority have a
right to act and conclude the rest." Unanimity of judgment is
never possible; and if action is to be taken, it cannot wait for
unanimity. The closer the judgments of the people approximate
unanimity, the greater the degree of consent secured for any
action or policy; but no government could ever operate upon
the principle of unanimity. How, then, are we to conceive of
rule by the majority of the people? Does it mean, as some contend,
that the will of the majority is to be regarded as sovereign, that
there is no appeal from that will, that its judgment is absolute and
unlimited? Is the rightness or wisdom of governmental policy
to be determined solely by the counting of votes? Does the
principle of majority rule demand that we abandon all qualitative
judgments in favor of a quantitative method? I do not think
so, and I think it would be dangerous to insist that it does.
If the principle of majority rule means that the will of the
majority must be conceived as unlimited and absolute, then it is
a principle, as the framers of our Constitution realized, that is
indistinguishable from tyranny. For the essence of tyranny is
unrestrained will—whether it be the will of one man, of several,
or of many. And the tyranny of a majority is no less cruel or
unjust—indeed, may be more so—than the tyranny of a single
individual. How, then, are we to conceive of rule by the majority
of the people?

What is demanded by the democratic form of government
is not submission to the will of the majority because that will is
numerically superior but rather submission to the reasoned judgment of the majority. We are obligated to submit to the decision
of the majority, not because that decision represents a numerically

superior will, but because it represents the best judgment of society with respect to a particular matter at a particular time. It is founded not upon the principle that the will of the many should prevail over the will of the few but rather upon the principle that the judgment of the many is likely to be superior to the judgment of the few. "For the many," as Aristotle declared, "of whom each individual is but an ordinary person, when they meet together may very likely be better than the few good, if regarded not individually but collectively. . . . For each individual among the many has a share of virtue and prudence, and when they meet together, they become in a manner one man, who has many feet, and hands, and senses; that is a figure of their mind and disposition. Hence the many are better judges than a single man . . . for some understand one part, and some another, and among them they understand the whole."[15] The principle of majority rule is founded upon the belief that the widest possible popular discussion and participation in the formulation of policy is likely to yield wiser decisions than a discussion limited to the few. The decision recorded by majority vote may then be fairly said to represent not a portion of society but the whole people.

And discussion and deliberation in a democracy are conceived as being continuous. While a majority vote is necessary in order temporarily to conclude a discussion and reach a decision, that decision remains open for discussion, and no decision is regarded as irrevocable. It always remains revocable in the sense that the minority is always free to continue the discussion and to endeavor to persuade others of the wisdom of its reasoning. The majority is not composed always of the same persons but is a fluctuating one, and the possibility always remains open for the minority to become the majority through the instruments of persuasion.

The majority vote does not precede the discussion but concludes it; it is the recording of a decision reached through deliberation and is not conceived to take the place of deliberation.

15. *Politics* iii. 11. 2–3.

To the extent that the discussion is not as widespread as possible, to the extent that judgment is coerced rather than persuaded, to the extent that the discussion is not carried on in as reasonable a manner as is possible, to the extent that it is used to obscure issues rather than to clarify them, to the extent that the participants make no effort to transcend the motivations of their private interests to contemplate the common good—to that extent the principle of majority rule is corrupted and debased. It is the reasoned judgment of the majority that obliges our compliance with its decision, not the will of the majority as such. To the degree, therefore, that rule by the majority becomes more an expression of will and less an expression of reasoned judgment, to that degree does it become less democratic and more tyrannical.

The democratic process is designed to determine by popular discussion and decision the choice of the best means to achieve the common good. In a recent discussion of the philosophy of democratic government, Professor Yves Simon has said:

> In essence, deliberation is about means and presupposes that the problem of ends has been settled. In the order of action, propositions relative to ends have the character of principles; they are anterior to deliberation and presupposed by it. The freedom of expression which is required by the democratic process of persuasion concerns all subjects that have the character of means and are matters of deliberation. Under fully normal circumstances the propositions relative to the very ends of social life are above deliberation in democracy as well as in any other system. Circumstances which make it necessary to deliver the principles of a society, its very soul, to the hazards of controversy are a fateful threat to any regime, democratic or not.[16]

He goes on to say that "a democracy may have to allow the questioning of the most indispensable principles" but such questioning is a grave sign of weakness and may point to the eventual disintegration of that society. "In democracy more than in any other regime it is a problem to assert principles in such

16. *Philosophy of Democratic Government* (Chicago, 1951), p. 123. Quoted with permission of the University of Chicago Press.

a way as not to jeopardize the free discussion of means, and to insure free discussion of means without jeopardizing the principles without which social life no longer has end or form. The risks proper to democratic practice demand that the assertion of principles be more profound, more vital, and more heartfelt than elsewhere. Unless this assertion is embodied in the living essence of community life, it will be nonexistent."[17]

Admittedly, the discussion in a democracy will never be completely rational, and private interests will always intrude themselves into any discussion of the common good; but a sound democracy will aim at achieving as rational a discussion as is humanly possible and at subordinating private interests as much as possible to the common good. This demands considerable self-discipline of both an intellectual and a moral character on the part of the individuals who compose the democratic society. It is the faith that such self-discipline is possible that makes democracy preferable to other forms of government that would restrict government to the few. The self-discipline that we expect of the adult in a democratic society has its roots in the early training of the child; and the kind of education, therefore, that we give our children, both at home and in school, may well determine the possibility or impossibility of democracy. The self-restraint that the adult must practice if democracy is not to degenerate into anarchy must grow out of the habits acquired in childhood. A child that knows no restraints, upon whom no discipline is imposed, is likely to grow into an adult who chafes at restraints and who is incapable of self-discipline.

Initially, the responsibility for developing good character rests with parents, for it is by virtue of their authority, which they may choose or not choose to exercise, that good habits are encouraged and bad ones discouraged. Virtue is acquired by the repeated performance of virtuous acts, and initially these acts must be compelled under authority. Not only will parents incul-

17. *Ibid.*, p. 124.

cate good habits of conduct, but they will encourage the habit of deliberation before action, and through formal education the rational faculty of deliberation will be trained to recognize the means by which human nature is perfected. This means that children must be taught the precepts of the natural or moral law much as we now teach the fundamentals of arithmetic or the rules of English grammar. If self-discipline is as essential to the preservation of freedom in a democratic society as is literacy, we shall not neglect the inculcation of moral principles any more than we would neglect to teach our children to read and to write. John Middleton Murry has said: "Just as the democratic society freely chooses its government, so the democratic citizen must freely choose to do his duty to the commonweal. He puts his conscience in control of his actions. He obeys the law, not as an external command, but. as the expression of his own better self, which wills to act in obedience to a law which its reason recognizes to be necessary. . . . Democracy is based not only in theory but in fact upon the reality of a universal obligation to obey the moral law. If that obligation is not recognized, and acted on, democracy must, in time of real stress, collapse. If the validity of the moral law is an illusion, so is the validity of democracy."[18]

But if we recognize the necessity for individuals in a democracy to strive to bring their thoughts and actions under the guidance of the moral law, we must not overlook the fact that the inherent defect of the human will to some extent will always thwart that endeavor. We must keep a balance between an excessive optimism about the motives of men and an excessive pessimism about their potentialities. Reinhold Niebuhr has written:

A free society requires some confidence in the ability of men to reach tentative and tolerable adjustments between their competing

18. "The Moral Foundations of Democracy," *Fortnightly* (September, 1947), p. 168.

interests and to arrive at some common notions of justice which transcend all partial interests. A consistent pessimism in regard to man's rational capacity for justice leads to absolutistic political theories; for they prompt the conviction that only preponderant power can coerce the various vitalities of a community into a working harmony. But a too consistent optimism in regard to man's ability and inclination to grant justice to his fellows obscures the perils of chaos which perennially confront every society, including a free society. . . . If these perils are not appreciated they may overtake a free society and invite the alternative evil of tyranny.

He suggests that it is "man's capacity for justice" which "makes democracy possible" and "man's inclination to injustice" which "makes democracy necessary."[19]

This is a very useful formula for understanding democracy, and it is one, I think, that the framers of our Constitution would have understood and approved. And none understood it any better than John Adams. Commenting upon the statement that "the people never think of usurping over other men's rights," Adams declares:

Is not a great part, I will not say the greatest part, of men detected every day in some disposition or other, stronger or weaker, more or less, to usurp over other men's rights? There are some few, indeed, whose whole lives and conversations show that in every thought, word, and action, they conscientiously respect the rights of others. There is a larger body still, who, in the general tenor of their thoughts and actions, discover similar principles and feelings, yet frequently err. If we should extend our candor so far as to own, that the majority of men are generally under the dominion of benevolence and good intentions, yet, it must be confessed, that a vast majority frequently transgress; and, what is more directly to the point, not only a majority, but almost all, confine their benevolence to their families, relations, personal friends, parish, village, city, county, province, and that very few, indeed, extend it impartially to the whole community. Now, grant but this truth and the question is decided. If a majority are capable of preferring their own private interest, or that of their

19. *The Children of Light and the Children of Darkness* (New York, 1944), pp. x–xi. Quoted with permission of Charles Scribner's Sons.

families, counties, and party, to that of the nation collectively, some provision must be made in the constitution, in favor of justice, to compel all to respect the common right, the public good, the universal law, in preference to all private and partial considerations.[20]

"Self-interest," he goes on to say, "private avidity, ambition, and avarice, will exist in every state of society, and under every form of government." Since they cannot be eliminated, it is necessary to control their effects. The only remedy is so to divide power that the selfishness of one group will check the selfishness of another and no one group, minority or majority, will have sufficient power to tyrannize the rest. The principle of the separation of powers, with its attendant system of checks and balances; the principle of federalism, with the division of power upon a geographical basis, were all designed by the framers of our Constitution to preserve liberty by making the concentration of political power in the hands of a few or of many a difficult, if not an impossible, undertaking. To this extent they realized that it is man's inclination to injustice that makes democracy necessary. The widespread diffusion of power is essential if that power is not to be abused. At the same time, they recognized that government exists to promote justice—in the words of Adams "to compel all to respect the common right, the public good, the universal law, in preference to all private and partial considerations." And it is this capacity of men to respect the common right, the public good, and the universal law, though they often need the compulsion of law to implement that respect, that makes democracy possible.

Under the influence of liberalism we undoubtedly developed too sanguine a view of the natural impulse of men to do good and consequently were plunged into despair when the liberal view of man was proved, by the force of events, to be too optimistic. In reaction to that view of man we have now come under the

20. John Adams, *A Defence of the Constitutions of Government of the United States of America* (3 vols.; London, 1787–88), III, 215–16.

tutelage of historical events to a more realistic understanding of man's propensity to do evil. Woodrow Wilson's hope that the world could be made "safe for democracy" seems now to have been naïve, though it did not appear so then; and in reaction to that optimism many persons now proclaim that the only reality in international politics is power and the self-interest of nations. Many intellectuals today not only underestimate the power of moral ideals but deny that moral ideals have any other role to play than that of rationalizing our private and selfish interests.

This reaction, however, may prove as devastating in its effects as was the liberal optimism from which it is the reaction. In correcting the errors in the liberal view of man, we must not discard the truth as well. To recognize the propensity in human nature to do evil is essential if we are to be realistic in dealing with the political and social problems that confront us; but if the recognition of the evil in man is proclaimed to be the whole wisdom about man, it will lead us to despair of man and to finding proximate solutions to our problems. A view of man that regards him as totally depraved is as one-sided and distorted as is the view which regards him as completely well-intentioned. A balanced view of man will emphasize both his propensity to do evil and his capacity to do good; it will not overestimate his motives, but it will not underestimate his potentialities. *Recognition of the sinfulness of human nature was never intended to paralyze man's capacity for intelligent thought and moral action but to liberate that capacity in the service of God rather than of self.* A balanced view of man will recognize the necessity for institutional checks upon the abuse of power, the necessity for law and coercion to restrain men from evil actions; but it will also understand that men are naturally attracted to the good, and it will seek to foster and develop this natural capacity. A balanced view of man will save us from the illusion that we can establish a political or social system which is perfect or make a reform which is final; but it will not despair of man's capacity for justice, and it will appeal to that capacity in seeking social change.

The degradation of man is amply attested to by the events of our time; and while we must be realistic in identifying the source of that degradation, the rebellious will of man, we require no lessons in despair. We know full well the depths to which men can sink. What we need to remind ourselves of are the heights to which men may climb. Under the influence of liberalism and the philosophy of the Enlightenment we believed that men could climb those heights alone and unassisted. That belief has now been shattered by the force of historical events. And many men, as a consequence, have been plunged into cynical despair. But we need not disparage the attractiveness of the heights or despair of men's approaching them if we remind ourselves of something the Age of Enlightenment forgot—that man is not an autonomous being but the creature of God, his moral weakness is his own, but his moral strength is born of the love of God. What the modern world has almost forgotten is the reality of spirit and its power; and history shows that it is the power of spirit that ultimately triumphs over material power, however great or formidable. The greatest empires and the worst tyrannies have ultimately come to an end, but the spirit of man has risen each time from their ruins to begin again the work of reconstruction. A contemporary writer has defined spirit as "the creative activity by which persons apprehend universal truth and good with rational insight and serve men with love born of faith in their divine potentialities."[21] This is the kind of spirit that has risen triumphant before in history and will again.

Democracy rests upon a faith in man as a rational, moral, and spiritual creature, and it is as much aspiration as it is fact. The ideals of democracy never have been and never will be achieved with perfection—they are goals constantly to be striven for but

21. George F. Thomas, *Spirit and Its Freedom* (Chapel Hill, 1939), p. 69. Quoted with the permission of the University of North Carolina Press.

never perfectly realized. In the last analysis, democracy is "a venture of faith in the moral and spiritual possibilities of men when entrusted with freedom."[22] Whether that freedom will be used to promote a just social order in which the moral and spiritual potentialities of all men equally will be encouraged to grow or whether it will degenerate into license and anarchy depends upon how each one of us conceives and uses it.

IV

Running throughout the history of Western thought there can be traced, broadly speaking, two competing conceptions of freedom, two competing philosophies of life. These two conceptions are represented in one of the Platonic dialogues by Callicles, on the one hand, and Socrates, on the other.[23] But each has had its counterpart in the life and literature of the Western world since that time, and the debate is one that continues in our own day. One regards freedom as the power to do what one wants; the other regards freedom as service to God and one's fellow-men. One regards power as an end in itself; the other as a means to promote justice and the common good.

The good, Callicles argues, is the gratification of desire, the pursuit of pleasure, and "he who would truly live ought to allow his desires to wax to the uttermost, and not to chastise them; but when they have grown to their greatest he should have courage and intelligence to minister to them and to satisfy all their longings." It is because the many cannot attain to this life and because they are ashamed of their weakness that "they praise temperance and justice out of their own cowardice." The truly great and noble man is the one who lives by the law of nature, which decrees that the weakest shall go to the wall. Might makes right is the first law of nature, and no man or society can stand up against it. In "reality" the ugly thing is not to commit a wrong or an injustice but to suffer one. It is the

22. *Ibid.,* p. 147.   23. *Gorgias.*

weaklings who have to "put up" with wrongs; and if we look at things as they really are, we shall see that it is the strong who invariably push the weaker aside. The right of the strong to impose their will on the weak, although contrary to conventional morality, is the first principle of natural morality. Callicles is convinced that "superior ability of any kind gives the moral right to use the ability according to your own judgment and without scruples. Hence he feels that in rejecting 'conventionalism' in morals he is not rejecting morality itself; he is appealing from a petty and confined morality of local human conventions to an august morality of 'Nature' or 'things-as-they-are.' "[24]

Callicles prides himself on being a "realist" and "a man of the world." The world of politics and of business has no need or use for the philosopher. Philosophy is for children, not for men of the world. Indeed, says Callicles, if I should see a man continuing the study of philosophy "in later life, and not leaving off, I should like to beat him . . . for such a one, even though he have good natural parts, becomes effeminate. He flies from the busy center and the market place, in which . . . men become distinguished and he creeps into a corner for the rest of his life." The world of politics, Callicles insists, is in need not of moral principles but of aggressive men who know that justice is nothing more than the will of the stronger. Such is one conception of freedom, and it is by no means confined to Callicles or to the fifth century B.C.

Socrates replies to the argument of Callicles by pointing out that the pursuit of pleasure itself is an endless pursuit and that the sensual desires of men are insatiable. The more we satisfy our desires, the more they crave, and our souls become like leaking casks that can never be filled. The impossibility of satisfying our desires shows the absurdity of the attempt. It is not the satisfaction of all kinds of desire without limit that men really

24. A. E. Taylor, *Plato: The Man and His Work* (New York, 1929), p. 116. Quoted with permission of the Dial Press.

want but happiness; and how is happiness possible without some rational principle in terms of which we can differentiate good pleasures from bad? A man who does exactly as he pleases in response to the desires of the moment is not a free man or a happy one but a slave to his passions, miserable in his bondage. He cannot truly be said to do as he pleases, for what he pleases is not within his rational control. If he would pursue that which is truly good for him as a human being, he must have some rational understanding of that good and exercise rational restraint over his desires.

Freedom consists not in the pursuit of pleasure but in a disciplined, ordered life directed to the perfection of that which is distinctively human. There is a good of the soul, just as there is a good of the body, and there is a science appropriate to each. The good of the body we call health, and the science of health is the science of medicine. It is this standard of health which the physician tries to reproduce in his patients. Corresponding to the science of medicine, there is a moral science which is concerned with the health of the soul. Just as the physician aims to produce a definite "order and regulation" in a human body, so the statesman should aim at producing "temperance and justice" in the souls of the citizens. Politics is a practical art which demands a knowledge of human nature and that which is its distinctive good. Citizens are not things to be manipulated but persons embodying ends in themselves—to minister to those ends is the distinctive art of statesmanship. Just as the physician's art depends for its successful practice upon a knowledge of the rules of health, so the statesman's art depends upon a knowledge of moral principles.

Callicles may be right in thinking, says Socrates, that the rule of life which Socrates prescribes is liable to leave an individual at the mercy of an aggressor, but he is wrong in thinking that life ugly. The "leviathan" says Callicles will kill you if you do not humor it. But Socrates replies that the important thing is not to live long but to live well. The dreadful thing is not to die but to enter the unseen world with a soul laden with guilt. No one, says Socrates, can escape Divine judgment, and before that judgment it is not the life prescribed by Socrates that will appear ugly but rather the way of life prescribed by Callicles.

Plato has described in the *Republic* how a society in which men allow their "desires to wax to the uttermost," who allow all desires free rein, at last succumb to a master-passion "as leader of the soul," which "takes madness for the captain of its guard and breaks out in frenzy." Tyranny, he shows us graphically, is the fruit of an undisciplined and disorderly life. Freedom conceived as the unrestrained pursuit of pleasure leads to slavery. The modern tyrants differ from the tyrants of Plato's day only by the fact that they have greater power at their disposal. They are not content to oppress men's bodies but endeavor by every modern technique of psychological coercion to coerce men's souls as well. "Under such circumstances the victory of Socrates over Callicles is not an academic question, it is a question of the life or death of modern civilization."[25]

25. Thomas, *op. cit.*, p. 125.

Index